TABLE OF CONTENTS

ACKNOWLEDGMENTS

I would like to thank Professor Saul David who manages the academic research MA in Military History at the University of Buckingham. He provided invaluable guidance, encouragement and support to me in the preparation of the academic dissertation which underpinned this book.

My archival research was conducted at the Imperial War Museum, London, at the National Archives, Kew and at the Liddell Hart Centre for Military Archives, Kings College, London. I would like to thank the staff at these institutions for their help, patience and unfailing courtesy.

Finally, I would like to thank my wife Deirdre, my children Tom, Alice and Robbie, and my uncle John for their support during my study sabbatical.

Abbreviations

AA & QMG: Assistant Adjutant and Quartermaster General
AG: Army Group
AFHQ: Allied Force Headquarters
AMGOT: Allied Military Government for Occupied Territories
CAO: Chief Administrative Officer
CIGS : Chief of the Imperial General Staff
CCS: Combined Chiefs of Staff
CMHQ: Canadian Military Headquarters
COPP: Combined Operations Pilotage Parties
COS: Chiefs of Staff
C-in-C: Commander-in-Chief
CTC: Combined Training Centre
DA & QMG: Deputy Adjutant and Quartermaster General
DC-in-C: Deputy Commander-in-Chief
DSD: Director of Staff Duties
ETF: Eastern Task Force (British)
FMC: Forward Maintenance Centre
GHQ MEF: General Headquarters Middle East Forces
IWM: Imperial War Museum, London
KCLMA: King's College, Liddle Hart Centre for Military Archives
JPS: Joint Planning Staff (British)
LofC: Line(s) of Communication
LofC Area: Line of Communication Area
LCA: Landing Craft Assault
LCI: Landing Craft Infantry
LST: Landing Ship Tank
NAPRW: Northwest African Photographic Reconnaissance Wing
POL: Petrol, Oil and Lubricants
RCASC: Royal Canadian Army Service Corps
REME: Royal Electrical and Mechanical Engineers
SNOL: Senior Naval Officer, Landing
TNA: The National Archives, Kew
WTF: Western Task Force (United States)

Glossary of Terms

Administration. The whole process of providing military forces with what they require or performing some service for them.

Assault Scales. Formations equipped so that they could penetrate up to a distance of ten miles from the maintenance areas on a beach.

Combined Operations. During the Second World War, the term 'combined' was used when two or more of the three UK armed services worked together.

DUKW. A two and a half ton amphibious landing vehicle manufactured by General Motors Corporation of the United States.

First Line Transport. The minimum transport capability that an assault unit needed to have available to it.

Forward Maintenance Centre (FMC). A location at the leading edge of a LofC, radiating from a base depot, where supplies, equipment and ammunition could be accumulated close to a battle front.

Joint Operations. During the Second World War, the term 'joint' was used to refer to operations or work conducted with other Allied nations.

Light Scales. Formations equipped so that they could operate up to a distance of thirty miles from the beach maintenance areas for a period of up to three weeks.

Line of Communication (LofC). A Line of Communication is the route that connects an operating military unit with its supply base and along which supplies and reinforcements are transported.

Line of Communication Area (LoCArea). A position on the LofC, organised under one authority for purposes of local administration. It might be divided into Sub-Areas which could function independently if the volume of work warranted it.

Logistics. Administration and Maintenance.

Maintenance. The process of keeping a military force in the field complete with personnel, materiel and providing a constant flow of reinforcement, supplies and stores from rear bases along lines of communication to the troops fighting in the front line. This process includes provision, holding and distribution.

Petrol, Oil and Lubricants (POL). A collective term which includes: aviation fuel, aircraft engine lubricating oils; motor transport fuel, lubricants; kerosene; diesel fuel; and petroleum spirit.

Second Line Transport. The transport capability, normally 3-ton trucks, which could move divisions or brigade groups and their ammunition and supplies.

Ship-to-shore. The transportation of assault forces from embarkation ports to a position just offshore target beaches, with troops then embarked on specialised landing craft for the short trip to the shore.

Shore-to-shore. The transportation of assault forces from embarkation ports directly to the target beaches.

Third Line Transport. The transport capability, normally under the control of an Army or Corps, for any purpose that circumstances might require.

War Establishment. The full wartime complement of personnel, equipment and vehicles for units and formations.

Preface

Operation Husky, the Allied invasion of Sicily in July 1943, was the largest and most dispersed amphibious assault of the Second World War. It was also the most complex combined operations logistics exercise attempted by the Allies up to that point in the war. An initial assault force of seven divisions, comprising 176,000 soldiers, landed across a one hundred mile span of southeastern Sicily.[2] Both the frontage of the assault and the size of the initial Allied assault force would be larger than that of the Normandy invasion just ten months later. Operation Overlord planners had fifteen months to prepare for battle, were able to assemble their invasion force from a home base and then faced a short sea crossing to France from a well defended shore. Operation Husky on the other hand was just five months in the making, was assembled from multiple locations across the Mediterranean and the armada needed to traverse two hundred and fifty miles of hostile, open water to reach the invasion destination.[3] Even so, the amphibious invasion of Sicily was a qualified success and beachheads with associated supply lines were established within hours of the landings to support the operational activities of the military forces. Although they faced an alliance of German and Italian forces, numbering in excess of 400,000 personnel, the island was successfully captured within thirty-eight days.

The preparatory period for Operation Husky, however, was chaotic and was described as a 'dog's breakfast' by General Montgomery.[4] Allied logisticians, already burdened with an immense organisational challenge, faced significant additional complications. Husky commanders were engaged in the war in North Africa until less than two months before the invasion date, leaving them precious little time to assist in planning. An inexperienced planning team, with a dysfunctional organisational structure, struggled to convene decisions. And it wasn't until 3 May that a final plan was agreed, just sixty-eight days before Husky D-day.[5] Despite the fact that logisticians were poorly served by an unstable and ever-changing operational plan, the largest armada that was ever assembled began to muster off the coast of North Africa in early July 1943. Significant logistical challenges had been overcome so that the assault force could be landed on Sicily. Ultimately, 467,000 Allied soldiers would be deployed on the island over the course of the campaign, fully equipped with the necessary materiel to successfully prosecute the campaign.

Given the immense scale of the amphibious invasion of Sicily, remarkably little has been written about the combined operations logistics associated with Operation Husky. Winston Churchill, writing in *The River War* in 1899, appealed to military students to be ever mindful of not ignoring the less glamorous, but no less crucial, aspect of military study that is logistics:

> Victory is the beautiful bright-coloured flower. Transport is the stem without which it could never have blossomed. Yet even the military student, in his zeal to master the fascinating combinations of the actual conflict, often forgets the far more intricate complications of supply.[6]

But academics have rather attributed victory in Sicily to the overwhelming Allied force and the lack of Italian and German resistance with no scholarly analysis on the role that logistics might have played in the success of the campaign. This approach to the reporting of the campaign by the official historians has been narrow and unsatisfactory.

This book sets out to addresses this gap in our knowledge. New insight is provided by extensive use of primary sources which indicate that the logisticians deserve significant credit for the role they played in the success of the campaign. Greater visibility is shed on the maturity, leadership and foresight they demonstrated in coping with the complications associated with a dysfunctional planning period. Their approach throughout can be seen to be prudent and framed within conservative operational safety margins. At the same time, they appeared willing to embrace innovation and

14

demonstrated agility and resourcefulness when faced with unforeseen challenges.

This work is an important and highly original contribution to our knowledge of the role of British combined operations logistics in the preparation and execution of Operation Husky. It asserts that logistics was, in fact, the defining factor in the capture of Sicily in August 1943 and that Operation Husky was a triumph of British logistics over immense odds and was a monumental achievement. Such an assertion necessitates a substantial revision of the accepted understanding of the role of logistics in the success of not just Operation Husky, but potentially of all subsequent amphibious operations in the Second World War. No connection appears to have been made to date between the combined operations achievements of Husky and the successful invasion of France in June 1944. And yet the D-day landings at Normandy were essentially trialled at Sicily when vital logistical and organisational foundations were established for the invasion of France just ten months later. Operation Husky was a defining event in the Second World War and it is hoped that this work will lead to a more balanced view of the role that British logistics played in winning the war in Europe.

Chapter One
Striking at the Soft Underbelly of Europe

When the Allies met at the Symbol conference in Casablanca on 14 January 1943, and agreed on the amphibious invasion of Sicily, they adopted the British Joint Planning Staff (JPS) Plan for Operation Husky.[7] It stated that the earliest possible invasion date of the island was 30 August 1943 and that the chances of success against a Sicilian garrison which included German formations was doubtful. It also forecast that, since forces would be drawn from across both ends of the Mediterranean as well as from Britain and the United States, planning would be complicated. To further compound the challenges, the first action of Force 141, the newly formed planning HQ for Operation Husky, was to put in place a complex organisational structure, based in ten separate locations.[8] While those challenges were significant in themselves, the Husky planning process was dogged by three additional obstacles. The first was that the principal Husky operational commanders were engaged in battle with Axis forces in North Africa right up to their capitulation on 13 May 1943 and so could only infrequently lift their heads from the current campaign to think about the next one.[9] Secondly, there was a lack of a full time executive commander, focused exclusively on the planning for Husky. Finally, neither the Symbol conference in January 1943, nor the Trident conference in May 1943, gave any specific direction for post-Husky activity, for instance an invasion of mainland Italy, and so the future maintenance needs of the armies was open to conjecture.[10]

These delays in establishing a firm plan created immense problems for the campaign organisers and it was not until 3 May that General Eisenhower, Commander-in-Chief (C-in-C) of the Allied Expeditionary Force, finally signed off on an agreed battle plan, just sixty-eight days before D-day. Despite the fact that logisticians were poorly served by an unstable and ever-changing operational plan, the largest armada that had ever been assembled began to muster off the coast of North

Africa in early July 1943. Two thousand five hundred and ninety vessels set sail from multiple locations across the Middle East and North Africa as well as directly from Britain and the United States.[11] Significant logistical challenges had been overcome so that 176,000 soldiers could be landed on the beaches of southeastern Sicily on 10 July 1943 with 14,000 vehicles, 600 tanks and 1,800 guns.[12] Ultimately, 467,000 soldiers would be deployed on the island over the course of the thirty-eight day campaign, fully equipped with the necessary materiel to prosecute the campaign.[13] Surprisingly, given the sheer scale of Operation Husky and the various challenges it faced, the logistics behind this monumental achievement have attracted limited scholarship. This would appear to be a serious historical omission and the role of logistics in the success of the campaign seems to have been completely overlooked. This study will examine the logistical challenges that were created for the British ETF by the lengthy and tortuous Husky planning process. It will analyse how successfully logisticians addressed those challenges in the administration of the Operation Husky campaign up to the landings on 10 July 1943. And it will assess whether the logistics of the British ETF was an important factor in the capture of Sicily on 17 August 1943.

Scope and Terminology

Operation Husky was one the largest military exercises ever staged and, in order to conduct an analysis of the logistics of the campaign with sufficient depth and rigour to make it academically valuable, the scope of this book has been necessarily limited. The amphibious invasion and the subsequent ground campaign were divided into two independent and separately maintained task forces, the United States Western Task Force (WTF) and the British Eastern Task Force (ETF). Each Task Force was a combined operation of naval and army forces but was separate and distinct from the other.[14] The airborne component of Operation Husky was conducted by a combined Allied command structure and is excluded from this study. By the middle of 1943, Britain had

been fighting Axis forces in the North African campaign for three years and its logistics structure was highly organised and its staff experienced. This book will therefore investigate the role that logistics played in the British ETF for Operation Husky from the Casablanca conference in January 1943, in the planning and execution of the combined operations landings on 10 July 1943, through to the end of the campaign and the reduction of the island on 17 August 1943. It is important to note, however, that at times British army and navy logistics will be viewed through an Allied lens as many aspects of the campaign were managed on a consolidated basis.

Two definitions are necessary in order to more closely define what is meant by the terms logistics and logisticians. This is especially important as the Allies used different terminology to describe broadly the same thing. Although widely used today, logistics was not a term that was in circulation in the British military during the Second World War. The process of supporting combat units was referred to as 'Administration' and 'Maintenance'. Brigadier C. J. C. Molony, the official British military historian of the Mediterranean campaign, describes administration as the whole process of providing forces with what they require or performing some service for them, and maintenance as the process of keeping a force in the field complete with personnel, materiel and providing a constant flow of reinforcements, supplies and stores from rear bases along lines of communication to the troops fighting in the front line.[15] Although confusingly Carlo D'Este, an American historian, writes that the British term administration equates to logistics in US parlance, this study will rather juxtapose and equate the American term logistics with the British administration and maintenance.[16] The term logisticians will be used to describe those individuals whose job it was to administer and maintain combat units. These would have been referred to as quartermasters or administrative officers in British military parlance at the time and, in the army, would have worked for Q branch.[17] Importantly they would not have had responsibility for the high level planning of a campaign.

Background to the Campaign

Plans in relation to an invasion of Sicily were refreshed by the British JPS every year from 1940 to 1943. The first of these plans was coded Operation Influx, was produced in London in 1940 by the JPS, and outlined an operation which envisaged scattered landings around the Sicilian coastline.[18] On 28 September 1942, the Prime Minister requested that plans be refreshed for a Sicilian invasion, and in a memo on 17 November 1942 to the JPS, Churchill expressed a desire 'to strike at the underbelly of the Axis in effective strength and in the shortest time'.[19] The Allies were at that point under significant pressure from Stalin to open up a Western European front to alleviate pressure on the Russian Red Army which was facing 85 divisions of the German Wehrmacht on the Eastern European Front. The Anglo-American invasion of French North Africa, Operation Torch, had been successfully completed the day before and Churchill wanted to ensure that he had firm plans to take to the forthcoming Allied meeting in Casablanca in January 1943. When Churchill, Roosevelt, their planning staff and their military chiefs met at the Symbol Conference in Casablanca on 14 January 1943, there was an undeniable momentum behind the Allies for the first time in the war. The British Eighth Army's exploits against the Afrika Korps in Egypt, bolstered by the success of the Anglo-American Operation Torch amphibious landings in French North Africa, gave the Allies 'a considerable degree of freedom in selecting their next move' rather than reacting to events elsewhere, as the official United States history records.[20]

Sicily did not initially present itself as the most obvious point of invasion entry for the Allies to Festung Europa (Fortress Europe) and the United States delegation, in particular, was nervous of over-committing to a campaign which would divert attention away from their preference, a cross-Channel invasion of Europe. Brigadier Ian Jacob, the Military Assistant Secretary to the War Cabinet, highlighted

these concerns with an entry in his conference diary on 14 January:

> The Americans…regarded the Mediterranean as a kind of dark hole, into which one entered at one's peril. If large forces were committed…the door would suddenly and firmly be shut behind one.[21]

The two delegations wrestled for days over how best to deploy their armies after the war in North Africa which, in January 1943, had an inevitability about its conclusion. As with most decisions the Allies made, a strategic compromise was reached. Neither delegation had an appetite for idle standing armies and ultimately the British, who were supremely prepared in their preference for an Allied assault on Sicily, prevailed in their arguments. The Combined Chiefs of Staff (CCS) therefore issued a directive on 22 January 1943 to General Eisenhower appointing him as Supreme Commander for what was in future to be designated Operation Husky.[22] Eisenhower was subsequently referred to as the Commander-in-Chief (C-in-C), rather than Supreme Commander, and the British General Alexander was appointed as his Deputy Commander-in-Chief (DC-in-C). Alexander would additionally be in charge of the planning and preparation of Operation Husky as well as commanding the Allied ground forces.[23] General Patton and General Montgomery would report to Alexander, with responsibility for the United States and the British ground forces, respectively. Britain ultimately had a clean sweep of the service command structure of Operation Husky with Admiral of the Fleet Cunningham and Air Chief Marshal Tedder appointed as Naval Commander and Air Commander respectively.

By early 1943, the British economy and especially the United States economy, were on fully established war-footings and were generating significant output in terms of the materiel of war. The Allies were now in the business of waging war by leveraging their combined industrial strength and implementing 'the new Allied policy of smothering the enemy

by weight rather than strategy'.[24] Delivering this enormous capability to the war theatres was going to be a significant challenge, however, and this would especially be the case for the invasion of Sicily. Operation Husky was the first action planned and executed by the Allies in the theatre of operation; Operation Torch, Operation Overlord and all succeeding expeditions, were conceived and managed by and in London and/or Washington. The invasion of Sicily would truly test the capability of the Allies not just to out-produce the Axis forces, but also to leverage their logistical capability in order to establish and effectively manage complex distribution channels and lengthy supply lines. Such an approach to war did not allow much flexibility though as every operation required planning down to the last detail. What one would have wished for in an operation as ambitious as Husky, therefore, with all the attendant logistical challenges and difficulties, was that at its heart would be an operational plan that was established at an early stage and which would never alter. This was not to be the case for the invasion of Sicily because of the complicating factors that have been outlined in the introduction.

The original JPS plan described an invasion which evolved over a number of days, was dispersed across the southern and eastern parts of the island, spanned one third of the coastline of Sicily, and prioritised the speedy capture of airports and ports as critical to addressing the subsequent logistical challenge of maintaining the armies in the field. The map in Figure 1 was issued on 10 January 1943 as part of the original JPS plan to illustrate where the various amphibious assaults were supposed to take place.

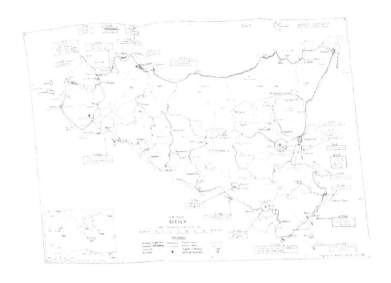

Figure 1
British Joint Planning Staff
Proposed Assault Map of Sicily, issued 10 January 1943 [25]

The limitations on the range of fighter planes ruled out the north of the island and the strategically important port of Messina as an invasion possibility. With fighter planes based on the islands of Malta and possibly also Pantelleria if that could be occupied, Syracuse, Catania and Palermo would just come into target range. Consideration of the concentration of forces on the southeast of the island had in fact been originally discussed by the JPS but was dismissed because it was assumed unworkable from a maintenance perspective. This view emerged as one of the key logistical findings from Operation Torch in November 1942 where it was stated that an amphibious assault plan should not rely on continuous maintenance over unsheltered beaches for more than twenty-four hours.[26] This pointed to the need to capture a suitable port within forty-eight hours of an amphibious assault and so the early seizure of Palermo, Catania and/or Syracuse was deemed essential in the JPS plan, together with the airfields of Comiso and Ponte Olivo. It was envisaged that the campaign would

then develop with General Montgomery moving quickly up the east coast of the island, reaching Messina as soon as possible and so 'shut the back door' in order to trap the Axis enemy between the British forces advancing form the south and the United States forces advancing from the west.[27]

From 12 February - when HQ Force 141 issued Planning Instruction No. 1, effectively the JPS plan with some minor modifications - until 3 May when General Eisenhower signed off on the final version, the operational plan evolved through seven stages.[28] Arguments and misunderstandings raged for months, exacerbated by the Tunisian war which dragged on far longer than was anticipated. This distracted all the principal Allied commanders from focusing on Operation Husky and was further complicated by the vast distances which separated the planning groups and the many battle groups. Each change threw up considerable additional problems for the logisticians, with existing plans torn up and replaced by new ones. At the heart of the debate were two conflicting but equally important issues: the early capture of Sicilian ports and airfields to secure maintenance advantage and the control of the Sicilian skies; versus the consequent dispersion of land forces and the risks that such a disposition posed. Eisenhower claimed to have never liked the original JPS plan and referred to it as 'assault by echelon', that is with each landing providing air cover for the next.[29] He was very concerned that the failure in one particular assault would cancel out the following ones and:

> we ran the risk of defeat in detail. Its complications, and successive rather than simultaneous assaults, were cited as risks outweighing the chance of defeat through lack of port facilities.[30]

General Montgomery was particularly critical of the planned dispersion of ground forces which would result in a huge gap between the WTF and the ETF and therefore an inability for the forces to cover each other's flanks. His letter on 12 April to Field Marshall Alan Brooke, Chief of the Imperial General Staff (CIGS), the professional head of the British Army,

clearly highlights his view:

> If you want to beat the Germans you have got to concentrate and hit him an almighty crack. Dispersion of effort is fatal.[31]

On the other side of the argument were Cunningham and Tedder who supported the capture of ports and airfields as critical priorities. Unfortunately General Alexander did not forcefully engage in discussions until late April and it was beyond the ability, and certainly the seniority, of HQ Force 141's head, Major General Charles Gairdner, to fashion a rapprochement in what had become by then an all-British impasse. When the protagonists finally sat together in Algiers on 2 and 3 May, time was running dangerously short, but it was at this point that Alexander made his decision, siding with Montgomery, and seeking and receiving General Eisenhower's support.

The final plan carried a significant risk, however, for unlike the British ETF which was scheduled to capture the port of Syracuse on D-day, the United States WTF would have no port which they could easily capture and would need to be able to maintain their forces over the beaches indefinitely. What swung the issue for Alexander and Eisenhower was the emergence of two significant innovations in over-the-beach maintenance: firstly, a two and a half ton amphibious vehicle, dubbed the DUKW, which was to revolutionise amphibious landings and maintenance capability; and secondly, a new organisational approach to beach maintenance called a Beach Group. Alexander says in his post-action despatch that he decided to 'take a risk on the administrative side rather than the operational risk of dispersion of effort' and comments that the DUKWs, which had only just arrived in North Africa for training purposes, were delivering on the claims made for them which were 'fully justified by their performance'.[32] With improved equipment and processes, logisticians were now able to markedly revise upwards their supply estimates for over-the-beach maintenance. Even so, safety margins would be

significantly eroded if the assault forces met with stiffer opposition on the beaches than had been anticipated and particularly if the Luftwaffe were able to carry out aerial attacks on the lodgement in its vulnerable early days and hours. Both Eisenhower and Alexander insisted therefore that the British ETF meet a commitment of providing 1,000 tons of supplies per day for the United States WTF through the port of Syracuse from D+14. This would supplement their own maintenance over the beaches until they could capture and bring into use the port of Palermo. While this final plan made sound tactical sense, one can imagine that with just sixty-eight days to go until D-day, it played havoc with the plans of hard-pressed army group quartermasters. Despite all these challenges, the invasion armada set sail in late June and early July, at different speeds, from many different locations across the Middle East, North Africa, the United States and the United Kingdom to converge on the beaches of southeast of Sicily. The ETF landed on schedule, at their designated beaches, XIII Corps at Avola (code-named Acid North, Acid Centre and Acid South) and XXX Corps at the Pachino peninsula (code-named Bark North, Bark South and Bark West) and the locations of the assault forces at 2359hrs on 10 July are shown in Figure 2.

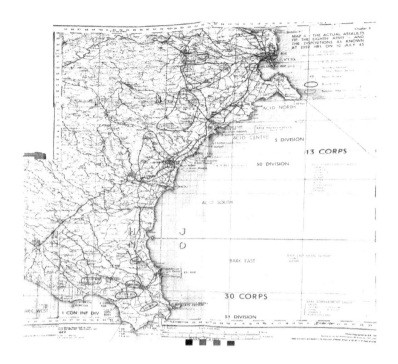

Figure 2
ETF assaults as at 2359hrs, 10 July 1943 [33]

One can only speculate whether the assault would have succeeded had the enemy put up a more determined resistance, but local coastal defences offered limited opposition and by the end of D-day the beach was secure, forces were moving inland, and the port of Syracuse had been captured. The consolidation of the beachheads between D-day and D+7 is shown in Figure 3.

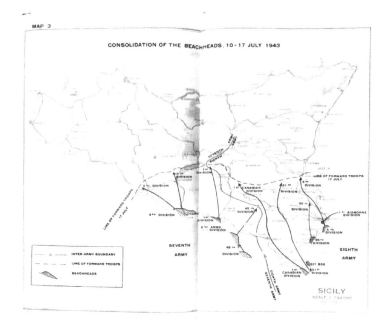

Figure 3
Consolidation of the Beachheads, 10 - 17 July 1943 [34]

Significant immediate maintenance shortages faced the logisticians however in the early period of the campaign. The supply convoys coming from the UK were attacked by German U-boats which created a supply crisis of troop rations, signal equipment and transportation. This situation was compounded by poor beach selection, which negatively impacted supply discharge volumes, and then the rapid advance of the ETF battlefront up to D+7. Nevertheless, these challenges were overcome by the impressive actions of the supporting services and well primed supply lines were quickly established to support the ETF.

It is not intended to describe every action of the ETF in the thirty-eight days it took to reduce the island of Sicily but rather to provide an overview of operational activities from a high-level perspective, so that the role that logistics played in the

28

campaign can be assessed. In summary, despite making good early progress from the beaches, the advance of the British ETF slowed as the German forces consolidated their position, setting up a Hauptkampflinie, or line-of-resistance, running from San Stefano on the northern coast, through Nicosia to the eastern coast south of Catania. This meant that they effectively abandoned western Sicily, shortened their front line and slowed the British advance. The American WTF, whose original task had simply been to establish a beachhead and hold station in order to protect the ETF's left flank, were let loose by Alexander on western Sicily where they quickly secured the ports of Agrigento, Trapani and then Palermo on 22 July. The Americans were then ordered to thrust eastwards along the north coast towards Messina as shown in Figure 4. The Hauptkampflinie is depicted as the line of forward troops.

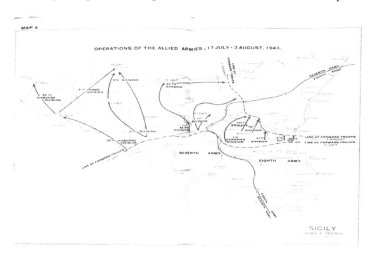

Figure 4
Operations of the Allied Armies, 17 July - 3 August, 1943 [35]

Albert Kesselring was the German commander in the Mediterranean theatre who oversaw operations in North Africa and Italy. On 27 July, he held a conference in Sicily where, acting on his own initiative which he admits made him 'persona non grata' for a while with Hitler, he told his local commanders to prepare to evacuate all German troops from the island.[36] In a series of masterful rearguard actions, the Germans used the rugged terrain of Sicily to their advantage and managed not just to evacuate their troops from Messina but also all their equipment and vehicles in one of the most successful troop and materiel withdrawals in military history. Both the ETF and the WTF staged attempts to leapfrog the retreating Axis forces in the closing days of the campaign with a sequence of amphibious landings. Unfortunately, they were unable to shut the back door before Axis forces escaped across the Straits of Messina to mainland Italy just three miles away. Although the Americans arrived into Messina just ahead of the British on the morning of 17 August, approximately 65,000 German and 75,000 Italian troops and their equipment had already been evacuated. The Allies had been 'out-Dunkirked' and those Axis forces which escaped were to form the backbone of the forces which contested future battles in the Italian campaign. Kesselring ultimately provided some important criticism of the battle tactics of the Allies and was particularly damning of their failure to capitalise on overwhelming resources. While he rated highly their logistical capabilities, Kesselring found the Allies ponderous and predictable on the battlefield. He stated that the Allies' 'strength lay rather in the vast amount of material they could squander' than in their tactical abilities.[37] The authors of many official post-action reports joined Kesselring in criticising Allied commanders for not being operationally more decisive. The final movements of the Allied forces up to the end of the campaign on 17 August 1943 are shown in Figure 5.

MAP 5

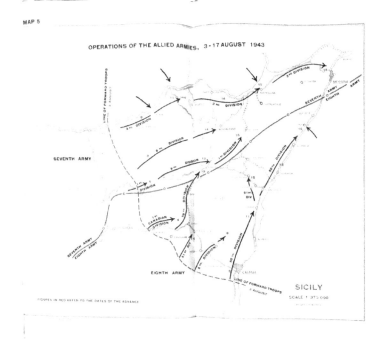

Figure 5
Operations of the Allied Armies, 3 - 17 August, 1943 [38]

Historiography

The invasion of Sicily has been the subject of serious academic debate from soon after the campaign right up to the present day. However, given the immense scale of the amphibious invasion, remarkably few publications look in isolation at the logistical challenges that the Allies faced, namely how troops and supplies were transported around the Mediterranean theatre to support and sustain the thirty-eight day campaign. This is surprising as Husky was the largest combined operations logistics exercise ever attempted up to that point in the Second World War. Although campaign administration and maintenance attract the limited focus of a handful of historians, the scholarship exhibits a tendency to skip quickly over some small logistical aspect of the pre-

31

invasion build-up and move quickly through the planning process to the embarkation of the armada and then to the campaign itself. Virtually every commentator covers the Operation Husky planning process and the events which delayed its completion until 3 May, just sixty-eight days before D-day on 10 July. Much has also been made of the atmosphere of mistrust and animosity that was said to have existed between the Americans and the British as they came together to prepare for Operation Husky and the supposed Patton/Montgomery rivalry is cited as evidence of this.[39] Historians also identify inter-service rivalry as being rife throughout early 1943.[40] Despite this, there is limited, if any, discussion as to how the planning delays and a less than collaborative atmosphere might have impacted the logistics of preparing for Operation Husky. This neglect has significantly affected a fuller understanding of the campaign. An examination of the outcome of the Husky campaign would suggest that in fact the Allies quickly became rather good at the business of organising war.

The secondary sources on the campaign can be roughly grouped into four categories: first, the official histories, which were published from 1949 to 1973; second, general works on Operation Husky; third, more detailed works which examine specialist topics of the campaign; and finally, a mix of academic theses, monographs and research papers.

The official military histories of the Second World War provide essential baselines for exploring Operation Husky, although they devote limited time to discussing campaign logistics. The United States was the first to complete its versions and the three key works here are: *The Army Air Forces in World War II (Volume 2 Europe: Torch to Pointblank)* by W. Craven and J. Cate;[41] *History of United States Naval Operations in World War II: Sicily-Salerno-Anzio* by S. E. Morison;[42] and *Sicily and the Surrender of Italy* by Albert N. Garland and Howard McGaw Smyth. Written in 1949, Craven and Cate's work barely mentions logistics in its narrative but devotes extensive time to addressing the criticism of the Air Forces which had begun to surface soon after the war as to their unwillingness to engage in Husky planning and integrate a tactical air plan alongside the army and naval plans.[43] This topic is important for this study as, if true, it had potentially far-reaching logistical consequences. Morison adds very little to our understanding of the logistics of the campaign, although he provides a brief insight into naval preparations for invasion, the training that was undertaken and a short section covering some of the new amphibious landing technologies that would be trialed on the Sicilian beaches.[44] Written in 1954, he added to the controversy with respect to the Air Forces by quoting General Patton in a conversation with Admiral Hewitt: 'You can get your Navy planes to do anything you want, but we can't get the Air Force to do a goddamn thing!'.[45] By the time the Army history is published in 1965, a better appreciation of the organisational challenges that faced the campaign had emerged and there was some attempt to describe the enormous war machine that was at work behind the scenes.

The key official British histories relating to events surrounding the Sicilian campaign are: *The War at Sea (Volume III, Part 1: The Offensive)* by S. W. Roskill;[46] and *The Mediterranean and the Middle East (Volume V: The Campaign in Sicily, 1943)* by C. J. C. Molony. Roskill's book was published in 1960 and is a detailed empirical account which contains comprehensive statistics on the composition of both the British and United States armadas as well as the challenges of getting all the craft, travelling at different speeds, to their designated disembarkation locations on time. Roskill neglects to focus, however, on the broader logistical complexity of the operation. Molony, the author of an inter-service history for the Mediterranean campaigns, admits in his introduction that many formations of the forces will go unmentioned in his narrative, especially the administrative services. He offers just 'a glimpse of this huge and complex subject' and pens a very short account of the administration and maintenance of Operation Husky. By 1973, it is clear that some understanding of the logistical challenges facing the campaign had emerged and Molony touches on topics such as the establishment of beachheads, lines of communication, the Army maintenance requirements, how Sicilian ports were brought back into use and how oversight of the administration of the campaign evolved through July and August. He summarises by saying that 'the administrative side of the campaign in Sicily is a story of well-earned success', but then says that this process was vast and 'our account must necessarily be restricted' suggesting that much more remains to be written.[47] The 1st Canadian Infantry Division also fought at Sicily and was part of the ETF under XXX Corps.[48] Its official historical officer, Captain C. P. Stacey, similarly admits that logistics had been overlooked and reports that:

> it was often impossible to make more than passing reference to the part played by the supporting arms, while less still was said of the administrative services...It is a very large field and no one arm or service can be treated in the detail it deserves.[49]

Alongside the United Kingdom Military Series of official histories, a Civil Series of work was commissioned and, from a logistics perspective, C. B. A. Behrens's *Merchant Shipping and the Demands of War* is illuminating.[50] She outlines the various demands that were made on the resources of the United Nations merchant navies in early 1943: servicing the needs of the war in the East, servicing the needs of the war in the West, feeding Britain, and preparing for Operation Husky. Pinch points had surfaced in available capacity which so alarmed Sir Alan Brooke, the Chief of the Imperial General Staff, at Casablanca in January 1943 that he decried 'the shortage of shipping' which had led to 'a stranglehold on all offensive operations'.[51] Behrens does not explain, however, how resources ultimately came to be freed up for Operation Husky and how logistical priorities were determined. This topic is in fact tackled with a little more detail in another official history, *Grand Strategy (Volume IV: August 1942 – September 1943)*.[52] The author, Michael Howard, states that naval vessels and air forces were in fact reassigned from the

Home Fleet and the United Kingdom based bomber offensive campaign respectively, running down the strength of domestic capability 'to the bare minimum compatible with safety'.[53] The resourcing of Operation Husky was turning into United States General Marshall's nightmare Casablanca premonition, that further Mediterranean operations would act like a 'a suction pump' drawing forces away from the main plot, the invasion of France.[54] Howard goes on to touch on yet another logistical challenge facing planners, the acute shortage of amphibious landing craft in early 1943, and how yet again resources had to be sucked away from the United Kingdom where they had been deployed for cross-channel training exercises.[55]

The first unofficial general work to focus exclusively on the Sicilian campaign emerged in 1962 and was written by Hugh Pond.[56] Pond served in Sicily as a Major in the British Army and therefore his account includes some primary evidence, though he has little to say about the logistics of the campaign. Pond's version of events is very Anglocentric and his account contains very little logistical detail. However, it is noteworthy in that it exploded the myth that Sicily should be viewed as a complete Allied success. In his conclusions, Pond controversially criticises 'the complete and utter failure of the Air Forces and the Navies to prevent the crossing of the German and Italian armies to the mainland'.[57] Although the official histories written up to that point had factually referred to the Axis withdrawal, they had not ascribed any blame for their escape from Sicily. Martin Blumenson, the American military historian, wrote *Sicily: Whose Victory?* in 1968 as part of the Ballantine's Illustrated History of World War II series and builds on Pond's premise.[58] However, it is disappointingly short on logistical detail and quite nationalistic, a nod probably to its intended audience, but it continues to undermine the view that Sicily was a complete Allied victory. Blumenson lauds the 'gigantic delaying action' of the Axis forces which 'kept two Allied armies at bay' and proposes that 'the German and Italian troops won a moral victory'.[59]

Arguably the most comprehensive and thoroughly researched analysis of the Sicilian campaign is *Bitter Victory* by Carlo D'Este, published in 1988. Although a United States Army Lieutenant Colonel, D'Este is neutral in his assessment of every Husky actor, having drawn on a significant volume of archival material in Britain, the United States and Canada. Many of his sources were new and his work has helped advance our understanding of Operation Husky. For instance, D'Este challenges the negative portrayal of the Patton-Montgomery rivalry and rather paints Alexander, the Allied DC-in-C, as weak and inept. In his summing up, he identifies Eisenhower and Montgomery as the only senior Allied staff who would subsequently admit that the opportunity for a decisive victory in Sicily had been lost. Others including Alexander, Tedder, Cunningham and Patton displayed a complete lack of candour by ignoring the unsatisfactory ending in their memoirs and biographies. D'Este concludes by suggesting that, although the Germans likened their escape from Sicily to the evacuation of Dunkirk, it was in fact a greater achievement. Unlike the British Expeditionary Force, the Germans escaped with their morale intact, fully equipped and ready to fight again as the Allies would later discover at Salerno, Monte Cassino and Anzio.[60] If there is a criticism of D'Este's impressive book, it is that his account fails to investigate how the planning fiasco, that he so clearly describes, could result in the subsequent logistical success of the amphibious invasion. We are left wondering how this gigantic enterprise ever came to pass without some other critical elements or forces at work. *The Day of Battle: The War in Sicily and Italy 1943-1944* by Rick Atkinson was published in 2007 and, although it covers the Sicily campaign only as part of a broader overview of the Italian campaign, it is a worthwhile addition to the Operation Husky scholarship.[61] The enormous scale of the invasion preparations is cleverly highlighted through a description of the ships' manifests as well as the complexity of the loading schedules, all of which had to be planned months in advance.[62] While his narrative is anchored in forensically detailed annotations, what he largely provides is a snapshot of the embarkation of the fully-loaded armada and he fails to discuss how this logistical feat was achieved. His account does not extend beyond a description of what would be required to support and sustain the troops in Sicily and is told almost exclusively from the perspective of the United States. Ian Blackwell's *Battle for Sicily: Stepping Stone to Vict*ory was written in 2008 and does little to improve our understanding of Husky logistics nor the campaign itself.[63] It is poorly researched, with little or no annotation, and his bold claims tend to undermine his credibility, the most fanciful of which is that the Americans saw Operation Husky as a 'time-filler'.[64] When it comes to analysing the Husky campaign from the Axis perspective, one work merits special attention. *The Battle of Sicily: How the Allies Lost their Chance for Total Victory* was written in 1991 by Samuel W. Mitcham and Friedrich von Stauffenberg. Mitcham and von Stauffenberg set out to 'tell the story of the Battle of Sicily primarily from the point of view of the Axis military commanders' and it is a welcome addition to our understanding of the campaign.[65] They propose that the Allies made a tactical mistake in the first place by deciding to invade Sicily, which was then compounded by a cautious and conservative approach which avoided gamble and risk. The Axis evacuation, termed Operation Lehrgang, is described in great detail and portrayed as a comprehensive German success.[66]

In the third group of secondary sources are a number of publications which, while providing more specialised insight into, and general understanding of, Operation Husky, offer very little extra information on the logistics of the campaign. *Supplying War: Logistics from Wallenstein to Patton*, written by Martin Van Creveld in 1977, remains one of the few specialist works to address the topic of wartime logistics and, while he devotes significant efforts to study the North African and Normandy campaigns, there is no mention or coverage of Operation Husky.[67] This is disappointing but, as he explains, hundreds of books have been written on strategy and tactics for every one book on logistics. He finds this genuinely surprising and quotes General Archibald Wavell 'The more I see of war, the more I realise how it all depends on administration and transportation' to drive home his point.[68]

Large scale airborne operations were still in their infancy at the time of Operation Husky and in *Drop Zone Sicily,* William Breuer describes four large exercises which had limited success: three of the exercises were parachute drops while Operation Ladbroke was a glider strike to seize the Ponte Grande bridge near Syracuse.[69] There has been detailed scholarly investigation of each mission and Dr John C. Warren, in a monograph entitled *Airborne Missions in the Mediterranean 1942-1945*, states that insufficient time was set aside for training and rehearsing each operation in advance.[70] For instance, all the transport planes used in the four operations had been requisitioned at the last moment. These had originally been assigned to transport ground troops to their points of embarkation across North Africa in the weeks leading up to the beginning of July.[71] This suggests that there was a clear breakdown in the quality of logistical preparation for these airborne exercises.

The final group of secondary sources are a mix of academic theses and monographs, similar to the aforementioned work of Dr. Warren, but these are invariably high-level, with no focus on logistics and with an almost exclusive focus on United States forces. One monograph is of interest, however, and was written by Stephen R. Cote in 2001.[72] A Lieutenant Colonel in the Marine Corps, Cote proposes that the logistics planning for Operation Husky overshadowed other operational functions. It became the 'proverbial tail that wagged the dog' and the over-emphasis on the logistical build-up on the beachhead prevented the Allies from incorporating speed and manoeuvre in order to create a fast, operational tempo.[73] This is an interesting theory and one of many which this book will seek to address. Finally, Trevor Stone in his dissertation, *Many Roads, Many Bridges*, analyses the logistical support of the British 2nd Tactical Air Force during the Allied advance from Normandy.[74] Stone decries the dearth of written material on the important discipline of logistics in the Normandy campaign and seeks to address this shortfall in his research.[75] If the better-known and more decisive Normandy campaign suffers from inadequate scholarship, it is hoped that this study can fill what appears to be a similar gap in our understanding of Operation Husky.

Conclusions from a Review of the Historiography

Given the immense scale of the amphibious invasion of Sicily and the combined operations challenges that were faced, remarkably little has been written about the logistics associated with Operation Husky. The academic focus of historians appears to have been drawn to other aspects of the campaign and the logistical challenges have been overlooked. While the complications of the planning process have been investigated, their collective impact on the logistics of Operation Husky has neither been quantified nor assessed. There is a clear need for a deeper analysis of British capability in this crucial area in order to establish a better balanced and more complete picture of the factors which affected the success of the campaign. This study draws on a number of previously unexplored primary sources in order to address what appears to be striking gaps in the way Operation Husky has been assessed and interpreted to date. It provides an important and highly original contribution to our knowledge, not just of the Mediterranean campaign, but also of the story of British army and navy logistics in the Second World War.

Chapter Two
A Dog's Breakfast

Immense logistical challenges were created by the tortuous planning process for the administration and maintenance of the British ETF in Operation Husky. The plan itself changed seven times in just four months and the final Husky plan was vastly different from the original JPS appreciation. This meant that the logistics of the campaign required much unanticipated work on the most fundamental administrative and maintenance aspects. In addition, the Husky command and planning structures, and their subsequent functioning, proved to be cumbersome and inefficient and created much unnecessary work for the logisticians. Complicating things further was the protracted nature of the Tunisian war, which did not end until 13 May. This had a serious impact on planning continuity as commanders wrestled with completing one campaign while preparing for the next. And, while politically expedient, the late inclusion of the Canadian divisions in the battle order of the ETF came with significant logistical consequences. This situation was then compounded further by an Allied shipping shortage in early 1943 which threatened at one stage to cause the postponement of the amphibious invasion. Overshadowing all of these factors, however, was the lack of any clarity as to what would happen after the island of Sicily was captured. Logisticians had to prepare for a whole range of potential future scenarios including an invasion of mainland Italy or invasions of Corsica and Sardinia. It is no wonder General Montgomery described the Husky planning process as a 'dog's breakfast' in a cable to Alanbrooke on 19 April.[76]

Evolution of the Operation Husky Plan

The original JPS Operation Husky plan, issued on 10 January 1943, was strikingly different in many ways from the final plan proposed by General Eisenhower and signed off by the CCS on 13 May.[77] And while every first draft of a plan needs to alter and adapt as new information comes to light, these changes were far-reaching and added significantly to the challenges faced by the logisticians. Consideration must also be given to the compressed time period in which these changes occurred. HQ Force 141 only began to examine the JPS plan from 12 February onwards, giving planners and logisticians less than three months in which to propose changes, have them accepted and then reset have logistics accordingly. The JPS plan envisaged a widely dispersed invasion, spanning a third of the Sicilian coastline, which evolved over a series of days and where the early capture of ports and airfields was deemed critical for the purposes of maintenance. The final plan was a concentrated beach assault on the southeast of the island, with an indefinite period of over-the-beach maintenance and no immediate capture of ports or airfields. The differences between the two plans are outlined in Figure 6.

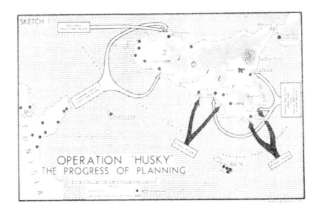

Figure 6
Operation Husky – The Progress of Planning [78]

Additionally, the JPS plan stated that 'We are doubtful of the chances of success against a garrison which includes German formations'.[79] The exact number of German forces based on Sicily at D-day, plus the number that reinforced the island through July, are not precisely known. Carlo D'Este analysed British, United States, Canadian and German primary sources and estimated German strength to have been up to 65,000 at its peak.[80] The Hermann Goering Division, 15th Panzer Corps, 29th Panzer Grenadier Division and 1st Parachute Division formed the backbone of the German defences, while the Luftwaffe rapidly moved their capability to mainland Italy as the invasion progressed in order to more effectively target the invading Allied formations. This number looks on the low side when compared with Alexander's official post-action despatch which reports that German forces, when reinforced after the invasion date, were 90,000 and that Italian forces numbered 315,000.[81] Either way, this was a substantially larger number of Axis forces than the JPS plan had anticipated. The JPS plan also materially under-estimated the shipping that would be required to transport Allied troops to Sicily. They had proposed that the invasion fleet would require 1,488 ships and landing craft. At the same time, they issued significant caveats as to the availability of shipping, and landing craft in particular. The invasion armada would ultimately comprise 2,590 ships and landing craft.[82]

The JPS regarded the capture of the island of Pantelleria, located just forty-seven miles east of the Tunisian coast and one hundred and eighteen miles southwest of Sicily, as a formidable task and they firmly advised in their plan that, as long as the Italian air base there was put out of action during the period of the Husky assault, its occupation was not an essential preliminary to the invasion of Sicily. However, Allied planners in late April 1943 began to view its capture as having undeniable tactical value, not least because of its 5,000-foot long airfield and a huge underground hangar but, more importantly, with the promise of total control of Mediterranean airspace. Operation Corkscrew was the plan formulated to initially bomb Pantelleria, followed by an amphibious invasion on 11 June. The island surrendered that same morning, soon after British commandos had landed, and valuable lessons were learned for the Husky landings just four weeks later which will be examined in detail in the next chapter.[83] Yet again, new challenges were thrown the way of logisticians as the original plan changed from its original form.

Weather was also discussed in the plan and, given the predictably benign summer weather in the Mediterranean, this was one of the few bright spots in what was essentially a gloomy plan. This was to prove to be an unfortunate oversight. Planners had assumed calm seas in which to launch an invasion fleet and put together the complex sequencing of embarkation times so that the fleet, all travelling at different speeds from many different locations, and including shore-to-shore landing craft with limited seaworthiness, could land at the same time.[84] However, by late afternoon on the 9 July, or D-1, the wind had reached a gale force of thirty-seven knots – force 8 on the Beaufort scale – and an unseasonably large sea with twelve-foot waves threatened to throw the armada off course. The Allied commanders paused to consider the consequences of postponement but decided to proceed despite this unexpected challenge to the prospects for the assault forces.[85]

In a clarifying memo issued to the Symbol conference on 21 January, based on a further examination of their own plan, the JPS concluded that the earliest possible assault date would be 30 August.[86] The Husky invasion would actually take place on 10 July. Finally, in what was to prove a prophetic understatement, the JPS authors ended their introduction with a note on planning which stated that 'Since the forces must be drawn from both ends of the Mediterranean and from outside, planning will be extremely complicated'.[87]

Administration and Maintenance Considerations

For what was going to be the most ambitious exercise attempted by the Allies up to that point in the Second World War, with open-ended arrangements as to how long they might need to maintain forces in a foreign field, precious little thought had gone into considering the logistics of Operation Husky, prior to the Casablanca conference in January 1943.

The JPS plan included some very basic details on the maintenance requirements of the invasion forces and covered just one and a half pages in a thirty-three page document. They estimated for instance that one division, including the build-up of its reserves, would require 500 tons per day and that one RAF squadron would need thirty tons per day.[88] Beyond that, there was no breakdown of the details of the cargo, the numbers of vehicles to be transported or the shipping space by volume that might be required to haul this tonnage. Some preliminary estimates of Sicilian port capacity were provided but, even with the early capture of the ports of Catania, Augusta and Syracuse, it was estimated that one and a half divisions would need to be maintained for the first month over the beaches, a situation which was described as 'presenting a major administrative problem'.[89] They also admitted that their calculations included only a small allowance for demolition by retreating Axis forces of port infrastructure but they did not discuss the impact of a more extensive Axis scorched earth policy or the impact of pre-invasion bombing by Allied air forces on other critical infrastructure such as airfields, roads, bridges and railways. At the same time, the JPS stated that they had scant information on the Sicilian beaches and their suitability to receive and sustain an invasion force, particularly details of submerged obstacles such as false beaches and lagoons, and that without this they would be unable to confirm whether and where forces could be successfully landed and adequately maintained.

The plan concluded by describing the feasibility of this operation as doubtful and that without more detailed study it was viewed as impossible to give a firm administrative opinion. This is quite a remarkable statement when one considers that an invasion was planned for mid-1943 and it betrayed a woefully inadequate understanding of the critical importance of logistics in an amphibious invasion of this magnitude. It was apparent that they had not consulted with any experienced quartermasters or logistics professionals in the many weeks they had spent preparing the report. So, as well as requiring significant reworking from a tactical perspective, which was covered in the preceding section, the plan that Force 141 was handed required an entirely new maintenance and administration foundation.[90]

There was a long list of things which the Husky logisticians were going to need to research and sourcing this information had a critical urgency in February and March 1943. First and foremost was information on which North African and Middle Eastern ports the armada would depart from. The transportation schedules for stores and troops, who would need to travel vast distances to their ports of embarkation, could only be determined when their destinations were known. Detailed beach reconnaissance would also need to be conducted over 300 miles of Sicilian coastline so that the optimal assault beaches could be graded, ranked and selected. Much of the coastline additionally has false beaches, where underwater sandbars present obstacles to shipping, and these needed to be identified together with the state and depth of the sea bottom and the slope of each beach. Mediterranean tides have a very low amplitude compared with many other seas and so it would not be possible to simply beach landing craft and then hope to float them off on a later high tide, something which was feasible at the Normandy landings for example. Consideration had to be given, therefore, to the total number of landing craft that might be needed for both assault and over-the-beach maintenance activities, assuming that many craft might become stranded. Various anchoring and pontoon innovations would need to be explored to ensure the instances of stranding would be minimised and that landing craft could complete multiple trips. Beaches also needed to be assessed for ease of egress so that mechanised vehicles could move inland to beach depots, and these in turn needed to be sited near roads so that LofC could be quickly and efficiently established.

The sequencing of the staggered departure times of craft from the United States, the United Kingdom and the various ports across the Middle East and North Africa, all of which moved at different speeds, would need to be estimated and then scheduled and each craft would require guidance to its own unique disembarkation point. Finally, the location and strength of Italian coastal defences would need to be determined so that troops could be landed in locations where higher concentrations of defensive forces or fortifications were avoided.

The terrain in Sicily would also present the land forces of the Allies with new challenges. They had fought a successful desert campaign in North Africa where mechanised forces could be deployed at scale on featureless and obstacle free battlefields. Sicily was mountainous with a rocky topography, cut by narrow valleys and dry watercourses and the Allies would be introduced to mountain warfare for the first time. The road system was under-developed with very little infrastructure in the interior of the island. As the official British historian commented, 'Sicily was a country where road-bound, mechanised forces were at a disadvantage, and where advantages lay almost wholly with the force which intended to delay and defend'.[91] War in such a country would present vastly different logistics and supply challenges to those of the desert campaign which the logisticians now needed to consider.

All but two of the divisions which were to compose the ETF in Sicily, were engaged in the Tunisian war until the end of the campaign on 13 May 1943 but there was a critical need for extensive combined operations exercises in order that army and navy forces could rehearse their beach assaults. Landing craft would need to be provided for training in particular for troops that would be landing in Sicily on ship-to-shore craft rather than shore-to-shore craft.[92] The broader maintenance requirements of the campaign would also need to be calculated: What reinforcements would be required and when? What rations would be needed and for how long? How much ammunition should be carried ashore in the first wave and what would be the replenishment rates that logisticians should apply? Casualties would also need to be estimated in advance so that measures could be put in place for the treatment of the wounded and the evacuation of the dead. Finally, the British ETF would move northwards from the landing sites into a low lying and swampy area to the West of Catania. Malaria was another enemy that required consideration, and precautions had to be considered to ensure the British forces did not become weakened by this most debilitating of diseases.[93]

The Allied commanders had a good understanding of the critical risk interplay between logistics and campaign success and this was demonstrated very regularly in the run up to the invasion. Montgomery sent a detailed personal diary note to the CIGS covering the period 23 April to 6 May, the time during which the Husky planning crisis came to the boil. Even though General Eisenhower had agreed to the final plan, Montgomery reports that 'The only possible snag was administration and this would now be gone into very carefully and so that a firm and final decision could be reached when General Alexander arrived on 3 May'.[94]

Major General Humfrey Gale, the AFHQ Chief Administrative Officer (CAO) who attended the critical 2 May meeting, wrote in his war diaries as follows:

> I expressed myself at the meeting forceably on the risks we were running in counting on beach maintenance as the sole method of supporting divisions in combined operations. However we may have to take the risk…It is, perhaps, time that we adopted a less satisfactory margin of safety since this is a hazardous operation and in any case we must take our chance on the maintenance.[95]

Both Gale and Montgomery would have also been aware that, as a rough guide, logisticians needed sixty-eight days to prepare a British division for embarkation and to be in all respects ready for battle.[96] By only furnishing the logisticians with a final plan in early May, the commanders were dangerously close to a point beyond which the invasion would need to be delayed.

Operation Husky Planning Structure

The CCS directive 161/1 to General Eisenhower, dated 23 January 1943, relating to Operation Husky, appointed General Alexander as his DC-in-C who was in turn 'charged with the detailed planning and preparation and with the execution of the actual operation when launched'.[97] From the outset, there was no doubt that Alexander had exclusive responsibility for both planning and logistics and he was directed to set up a special operational and administrative staff, with its own Chief of Staff, for planning Operation Husky and establishing all the necessary contingency plans. The official British historian surmises that the CCS rationale behind the creation of a special staff for operational and administrative planning was driven by their concern that Husky commanders 'in particular Eisenhower, Alexander, Montgomery, and Patton, were deep in the day-to-day conduct of the campaign in Africa and would continue to be until the middle of May'.[98] The first meeting of the Operation Husky planning staff took place on 10 February in Room 141 of the St. Georges Hotel in Algiers and so HQ Force 141 came in to being. It was provided with offices at the Ecole Normale at Bouzarea, just outside Algiers as all AFHQ accommodation was already overcrowded.

The origins of the Operation Husky planning complications began with these CCS campaign directives and the interplay with the existing structure of high command in the Mediterranean. AFHQ had been established in late 1942 to control all Allied operational forces in the Mediterranean theatre of war. Given that Eisenhower was the C-in-C of AFHQ, it does seem unusual in retrospect that the CCS did not invest his command structure with planning and execution responsibility for Operation Husky. Eisenhower was 'infuriated' with the CCS Husky command directives when he received them and the 'intrusion of the British Committee system in the AFHQ scheme of things'.[99] He favoured a structure where a single commander exercised executive control over tactical and operational matters. He had been effectively kicked upstairs and elevated to a chairman role, presiding over a committee made up of a triumvirate of British commanders who exercised executive authority. Those commanders were not all co-equal, however, and the executive structure contained an inherent design fault. Although Alexander, Cunningham and Tedder had equivalent operational responsibilities for the Army, Navy and Air forces respectively, Alexander was super-omnia in that he was DC-in-C but also responsible for planning and execution. Not only did this create a clear conflict of interest between himself, Cunningham and Tedder, it also created a strange working relationship with Eisenhower. It is apparent that whether because of the command structure, the distraction of the Tunisian war or the distance separating them, their relationship was not strong and was in an early stage of evolution. In fact, matters nearly came to an ugly head at the beginning of April when the CIGS forwarded a letter to Churchill that he had received from Alexander which clearly highlighted how poor the communication was between them. Churchill responds to the CIGS on 6 April when he writes:

> This correspondence is remarkable as showing the relations between Eisenhower and Alexander. After the battle is over I shall ask Alexander to keep his Chief more fully informed. There would be an awful row if Eisenhower's message ever saw the light of day. So much depends on going through the ceremonial processes.[100]

So much for the upper echelons of high command. But what were the implications for the management and accountability of the logistics of Operation Husky? The official history of AFHQ says that the difference in the American and British systems of administration proved too great to allow either to adopt the other's system.[101] It was therefore decided that the administrative side of AFHQ should incorporate whatever separate American and British organisations were necessary to operate their respective systems but coordination was affected under the direction of the CAO, who throughout 1943 was the British Major General Humfrey Gale. While AFHQ was an integral component of the logistics structure, as we shall see in the next chapter, their involvement in Operation Husky planning matters was essentially non-executive and they were at best a peripheral overseer, although the exact lines of demarcation could best be described as blurred.[102] Gale's war diaries highlight what a difficult situation this created and what a demanding task he had in making sure that he was in a position to exert administrative influence over planning, and thereby ensure everything stayed on schedule.[103]

Given this complicated backdrop, Force 141 was cast as the pivotal unit in Operation Husky, a position which was not optimal and which the organisational designers among the CCS could never have envisaged. Force 141's influence only extended, however, to outline planning and to the coordination of detailed planning for the campaign. Although integrated with Anglo-American staff, it was organised on the British staff system which added further challenges, as each tradition had different ways of managing and planning military affairs. At first, and to complicate matters even more, Force 141 worked as a sub-section of AFHQ's G-3 branch which had responsibility for operations, including staff duties, exercise planning, training, operational requirements, combat development and tactical doctrine. It always regarded General Alexander as its responsible executive, however, and it formally disengaged from AFHQ on 13 May, at the end of the Tunisian war, when it joined Alexander's Fifteenth Army Group as an independent operational HQ. The more detailed operational planning for Husky on the other hand was the responsibility of the ETF and WTF commanders who established Force 545 in Cairo and Force 343 in Casablanca respectively to manage their task force logistics. An added organisational wrinkle for the British Force 545 was that they also needed to liaise with the War Office in London and General HQ Middle East Forces (GHQ MEF) in Cairo with regard to the mounting of the division which would sail directly from the United Kingdom to Sicily. The command relations of HQ Force 141 with the other HQs is shown in Figure 7.

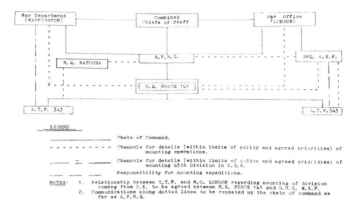

Figure 7
Command Relations of HQ Force 141 with other HQs,
April 1943 [104]

Further complications existed owing to the wide dispersal of the various planning and battle groups. The CCS had prescribed a system of unified command for combined United States-British operations in CCS 75/3, on 24 October 1942 which is detailed at Appendix A. Eisenhower's command structure for Operation Husky followed this approach closely, with one extremely important logistical exception: point eleven stated that the land, naval and air commanders must carry out their duties at the headquarters of the C-in-C. This directive was essentially ignored by Eisenhower in Operation Husky - the commanders were not co-located - and it created significant inter-service coordination challenges in the coming months. In fact, Admiral Cunningham in his post-action despatch on the invasion of Sicily, said 'The separation of the Commanders…was manifestly undesirable and might have proved extremely awkward had things begun to go awry'.[105]

The various HQs involved in preparing for Husky were

dispersed across ten locations in North Africa, as well as in Washington and London, and the distances between them were immense.[106] For instance, Rabat and Cairo were 4225 km apart and such a complex planning structure required active additional shuttle diplomacy. One of the main difficulties of coordinating matters when such vast distances existed were regular incidents of 'trivial misinterpretation' whereby, although the various groups were far apart by air, they were perhaps almost too closely linked by wireless and cable: 'For good communications often favour debate instead of hastening decisions.'[107]

The challenges that such distances posed for decision-making are seen by analysing Major General Gairdner's travel schedule, from his arrival as head of Force 141 in North Africa on 20 February, to the tendering of his resignation on 3 May. He took twelve long distance flights during that period, nine to visit Alexander at his HQ in Constantine which was over 440 km away. He also visited Malta, Cairo and London, and spent a total of thirty-two days away from the Force 141 base in Algiers, nearly half of the total time he was in charge of that group. When this travel requirement and consequent disruption is multiplied across the broader Husky planning teams, the challenges of distances become painfully apparent.[108]

Major General Charles Gairdner arrived in Algiers from India on 20 February to become the Chief of Staff of Force 141. Gairdner had had a relatively undistinguished military career up to that point and was as short of combat experience as he was of planning and logistics expertise. His personal war diary paints him as an arch-delegator and it is apparent from his entries in late February that he has serious personal doubts about his own fitness for the job.[109] His lack of seniority and an uncharismatic personality meant that Force 141 punched well below its weight at the key decision-making junctures in the planning process. Given the vacuum created by the virtual absence of Gairdner's seniors from Husky planning until late April, the enormous physical distances between the various planning and battle groups, and the cumbersome way in which the Husky planning structure had been constructed, it is arguable whether anyone could have been more successful in the role. Even so, he attracts criticism early on from the AFHQ CAO following a meeting on 2 March where Gairdner seems to be more concerned about issues such as his accommodation and other amenities. Gale writes in his diary that Force 141 needs to rather focus on the job at hand and 'realise that they are on active service…and it is simply a matter of getting the show properly organised'.[110] Gairdner also appears to have been found guilty of a tendency for empire-building. When Gale chaired a meeting on 20 April to discuss the War Establishment of Force 141, he wrote in his diary that '141 had produced a ridiculous establishment of over 400 officers which bore no resemblance to my picture of what it should be…This was a useful meeting as it put 141 on the rails'.[111]

In hindsight, HQ Force 141 should have been established with a less complicated reporting structure, with significantly more AFHQ involvement in planning and logistics and, most importantly, with a more senior ranking officer in charge. It is interesting to note that the planning structure for Operation Overlord, which was established in March 1943, was led by a Lieutenant General and reported directly to the Supreme Allied Commander, avoiding the seniority and line-management challenges which Operation Husky grappled with.[112] General Montgomery also became increasingly critical of both Gairdner and Force 141 and, in a letter to the CIGS on 23 April, he suggested that Gairdner needed to be replaced:

> Force 141 is a completely theoretical planning staff. The head of it, Major-Gen Charles Gairdner, is not up to it; he does not know the battle repercussions; he is a bundle of nerves; he inspires no confidence. The whole atmosphere is far removed from war, and they produce work that has no relation to the practical realities of battle.[113]

In any case, Gairdner tendered his resignation on 3 May and was replaced by Major General A. A. Richardson. So, at a critical moment in the preparations for the invasion of Sicily, there was further disruption with a change in the leadership of the principal planning and logistics coordination unit.

Gale was concerned with even higher matters, however, namely the overall administration of the Mediterranean Theatre, before, during and after Operation Husky. As the centre of gravity of the Mediterranean campaign moved from North Africa to mainland Europe through the early summer of 1943, so too the responsibility for the maintenance and administration of the Allied war machine needed to change. This dynamic is of importance to this study as it was to have implications for how the LofC would be established in Sicily, who would be responsible for it and the challenges that would face logisticians with the uncertainty as to post-Husky activities. Alexander's Eighteenth Army Group attempted to centralise the control of the logistics of the Allied ground forces by absorbing Force 141 from AFHQ G-3 into its own staff office on 13 May 1943. This ran counter to the original principles of the Allied command structure and relationships between the AFHQ and Alexander's staff officers became contentious.

Absentee Commanders

When the Allies set in motion the Operation Husky plans in January 1943, they forecast that the war in North Africa would be over by the end of April. This timetable would ensure senior commanders could work with planners to evolve the Husky plan as well as allowing ample time for assault training and the logistical preparations for the invasion of Sicily. However, the Axis forces fought bravely in Tunisia, and on a broad front, surrendering only on 13 May. This had a significant impact on the senior Allied commanders who were distracted and preoccupied by one battle while trying to prepare for the next one. In addition, all but two of the Allied divisions which were to fight in Sicily were engaged in the Tunisian war. Time which should have been available for resting battle-weary troops, repairing and recycling armaments and moving personnel and stores to the Husky embarkation ports, was rather spent in battle.[114] The impact of this on the administration of the campaign, and in particular pre-invasion training, will be discussed in the next chapter.[115]

It is debatable whether a different group of individuals in a different leadership team would have been done a better job, given the circumstances. In correspondence with the CIGS on 19 April, Montgomery crystallises the problem that all the Allied commanders faced: 'I'm fighting hard to get some sanity into the planning. It is hard work; and I'm also fighting the Germans - which is much easier.'[116]Alexander is remarkably honest on the opening page of his official Sicily despatch when he says that, owing to his responsibility leading the armies in the North African campaign, 'it was not possible for me to take direct control immediately of the planning of the operations'.[117] Even as late as 5 April, he confides to the CIGS that he has had too little time to 'study the technical side of combined operations'.[118] This is a disturbing admission from a commander who had sole planning and execution responsibility for the largest amphibious exercise ever undertaken and it demonstrated an inability to master the detail of the plan, to impose a direction on the situation and to delegate appropriate responsibility.

Concerns were being felt among Alexander's colleagues too and on 1 April General Maitland-Wilson, the British C-in-C Middle East, wrote to the CIGS: 'It would appear planning in Algiers is suffering from lack of a full-time commander on the spot and you may wish to send someone out there to sort things out.'[119] Never shy of criticising his superiors, but also clearly exasperated by the original Husky plan which he felt was foisted on him and the other fighting commanders, Montgomery wrote to the CIGS on 12 April 1943:

> 18 Army Group ought to be sitting back and controlling the battle in its bigger aspect; they ought also to be giving very clear and definite directions about Husky. But they don't do so…There is a lack of 'grip'. The Husky planning is in hopeless mess…We

have made such a mess of it so many times in this war that it makes me quite angry to see us drifting the same way now.[120]

And on 6 May, he writes again to the CIGS with what appears to be further criticism of Alexander:

> I am struggling hard to make a success of Husky. It is a most trying business, because there is no one to look to; I hope we will never again adopt the principle of the 'absentee commander'. It has been a dismal failure and has all but landed us right in the soup.[121]

Undoubtedly, Alexander must take a significant portion of the responsibility for the Husky planning mess as the CCS directive made him uniquely accountable for the planning, preparation and execution of Operation Husky. Too often he let matters drift, dodged critical decisions and as Gairdner confided to his war diary 'on no single occasion either backed me up or made an independent decision of his own'.[122]

Ultimately it was Eisenhower who stepped in to sort out what had become, in early May, an 'unseemly British inter-service dispute', with Cunningham and Tedder diametrically opposed to the changes that Montgomery had proposed to the final version of the plan.[123] However, Eisenhower cannot emerge from this period without some measure of shared blame, despite the cumbersome command structure he had been presented with. It is telling how difficult it was for Gairdner to get time with him to discuss Operation Husky during the planning period. After his first official Husky meeting on 22 February, Gairdner wrote in his war diary that Eisenhower appeared to be harassed by the magnitude of his job and had made it abundantly clear to him that at that moment he did not want to be worried with Husky.[124] In fact, Eisenhower is absent from the majority of Husky planning sessions and only intervenes at some of the major decision-making moments. This would ordinarily be forgivable if everything had been proceeding smoothly with the campaign preparations, but this was not the case and, given Eisenhower's undeniable skills and experience as a planner and administrator, his absence from the Husky picture is all the more mystifying. General Omar Bradley, who led XXX Corps/Army under General Patton in the WTF, reflected in his memoirs that:

> Ike must…share a large part of the blame…Inasmuch as his three deputies were absorbed in the Tunisia fighting, it seems to me that it was all the more important that Ike give the Sicily operation his utmost care and attention. He was the logical man to conceive the operation as a whole, impose his imprint, see it through, and accept responsibility for the consequences. But Ike did not rise to the challenge.[125]

The official British historian concurs, without pointing fingers, and suggests that 'it was this absence of a full-time executive commander, free from other commitments, which be-devilled the planning and created the doubts, uncertainties and delays which so confused the issues' and goes on to suggest that it was remarkable under the circumstances that an agreed plan was formulated at all.[126]

Although it is probably going too far to suggest that Eisenhower and Alexander should be charged with a dereliction of collective duty and responsibility, they made the fatal mistake of issuing the JPS document as their preliminary plan in early February. As neither had properly studied it nor resolved its inherent weaknesses, it was treated as a proposal for debate rather than as a commander's diktat, and confusion reigned.[127] Finally, it is clear also that they were both aware of the deteriorating situation on the planning front in April but did little to address it, ultimately threatening the success of the invasion of Europe.

The Canadians in Sicily

The very late substitution of UK-based Canadian forces in

place of the British 3rd Division in the Husky battle order caused an immense additional logistical headache for the War Office in London and for the logisticians of the ETF in the Mediterranean. Canadian troops had been in England since 1940. Yet they had been assigned to training and guard duties along the south coast and, with their morale low, had gained a reputation for being unruly wherever they were based. Although 5,000 men of the 2nd Canadian Infantry Division had comprised a significant part of the ill-fated attack on Dieppe in August 1942, this was viewed as merely a large raid rather than a campaign, and the Canadian public questioned the wisdom of sending an all-volunteer Army overseas just so they could guard the borders of the mother country. The Canadian Prime Minister, William Mackenzie King, put pressure on Churchill to find better use for the Canadian army and participation in the invasion of Sicily seemed to offer a good solution.[128] However, the British 3rd Division had already been selected for the assault and had been engaged in a programme of invasion training for some time. Churchill acquiesced but it wasn't until 27 April that the Canadian Government approved the deployment of the reinforced 1st Canadian Infantry Division to Operation Husky, comprising 1, 2 and 3 Canadian Infantry Brigades and the 1 Canadian Army Tank Brigade.[129] The senior Canadian formations in the United Kingdom, left with just over two months for training and planning, lost no time in getting involved and a handover meeting took place on 25 April at Norfolk House in London with the now relegated British 3rd Division where each 3rd Division head handed over its Operation Husky file to a Canadian counterpart in an exercise badged Operation Swift.[130]

To make matters even more challenging, the senior Canadian military officer, Major General Salmon and a number of his senior Canadian staff officers, were killed in a plane crash near Barnstaple on 29 April 1943 as they to flew to Cairo to begin Husky planning.[131] Major General Simmonds was appointed as Salmon's replacement and arrived in Cairo on 1 May, but very soon a series of maintenance and administration challenges arose. First, there were problems in organising reinforcements for the Canadian assault force where immediate casualties were to be expected, and then deciding how those troops would be deployed. British forces would be reinforced from existing troop pools in the Middle East but there was no Canadian representation in the theatre and to mobilise Canadian reinforcements in late May, and set them up in depots close to the theatre of operation, risked compromising security.[132] The solution finally agreed upon was that reinforcements would travel in the D+3 convoy. Secondly, the lack of shipping space made it necessary to reduce the number of Canadian administrative units on board who would be responsible for maintaining and repairing Canadian vehicles. These differed in many respects from British vehicles, particularly with respect to spare parts, but it was nevertheless decided to use Canadian vehicles only for the 1st Canadian Infantry Division. Finally, much equipment of Canadian manufacture, including sub-machine guns – the Canadians used the Sten gun, the British used the Thompson – was replaced by equipment of British manufacture and on British scales.[133] Although the Canadians had just taken delivery of the latest in wireless equipment, they needed to adopt more dated British wireless equipment as they would be a division which would be operating in a British corps. This they did but it necessitated extensive additional last-minute training.[134] While these measures eased some of the future maintenance issues, the introduction of the Canadians this late in the planning phase piled more challenges onto the already stretched Husky logisticians.[135]

Shipping

Shipping in the Second World War has been described as the sine qua non of logistics 'the arterial link between the productive heart in the United States and the fighting organs in the theatres'.[136] The shortage of shipping in the first six months of 1943 was the most critical element in the uncertain picture that the JPS planners outlined for the prospects of a successful Sicilian invasion, and it was the one with possibly the most far-reaching implications. So alarmed was the CIGS at the Casablanca conference that he decried 'the shortage of shipping' which was leading to 'a stranglehold on all offensive operations'.[137] The great question at Casablanca was deciding what proportion of the Allies' shipping resources should be devoted to the war in the East and how much to the war in the West. As early as 26 February, however, Admiral Ramsay, who would command the ETF naval formations, realised that the planners had grossly under-estimated the shipping required for the British portion of the invasion of Sicily. As a consequence, the early maintenance requirements were larger than could be met by the allotted shipping, even before the Husky plan had been revised in March to include an extra British division.[138] The full extent of the global shipping problem became clearer on 18 March 1943 when Churchill asked Lieutenant General Ismay, the chief staff officer on the COS committee, to quantify the extent of the shipping shortage.[139] Lord Leathers, the Minister of War Transport, was asked to respond and confirmed that Britain would not be able to rely on American ships in the volume that had been previously estimated.[140] In the end, the United States Navy agreed to make ten additional ships available to the ETF but these did not fill the entire gap.

The projected Husky shipping needs had already run down the strength of the United Kingdom Home Fleet to the bare minimum compatible with safety; HMSs *Nelson*, *Rodney*, *Warspite* and *Valiant* would be joined at Sicily by two more battleships.[141] It was at this juncture that the stringent shipping shortage precipitated a revision of the overall Allied strategy. The Casablanca conference had held out the hope of a cross-channel invasion of Europe in 1943, Operation Bolero, and Churchill in particular was keen that it should remain on the table. However, the shipping demands of Operation Husky could only be met by drawing more deeply on the reserves of the United Kingdom and specifically those assault landing craft which had been earmarked for Bolero training and for cross channel operations.[142] His Chiefs of Staff and the CIGS finally made it clear to him on 11 April that he must reconcile himself to a purely Mediterranean strategy in 1943.[143] This determination, and the consequent shipping implications, was made very late in the countdown to Husky and necessitated a significant movement of British naval craft from the United Kingdom to the Mediterranean.

Lack of Post-Husky Clarity

It seems remarkable that the Allies had no firm plans in place for what they would do after the conclusion of Operation Husky, even as the invasion armada sailed for Sicily. To move an army with close to half a million men across a vast expanse of sea, stretching supply lines further than had been the case thus far in the Second World War, and without any idea of next steps, appeared to be foolhardy in the extreme. This lack of clarity stemmed from a deficit of fulsome support for the invasion of Italy on the part of the United States at the Symbol conference at Casablanca in January 1943. Prior to that conference, it had actually taken quite some effort on the part of the British CIGS, to convince his own JPS that Sicily rather than Sardinia was the only objective in the Mediterranean worth targeting. It was Prime Minister Churchill who swung the British delegation to a Sicilian invasion when he referred to the proposed capture of Sardinia as 'that piddling operation'.[144] The challenge now was to convince their United States allies of the merits, not only of the invasion of Sicily, but of any further involvement in the Mediterranean theatre when the North African war was ended. Led by President Roosevelt, the Americans favoured an invasion of northern France as the better European action but, over the course of a number of days, the CIGS and Sir John Dill, the Chief of the British Joint Staff Mission in Washington, convinced the Americans of the merits of the Sicily enterprise. Rather than overplay their hand, the British delegation decided not to table a discussion on post-Husky operations once the Sicilian invasion had been agreed. Operation Husky was therefore viewed at the time as an end in itself and the failure to provide General Eisenhower with a mandate for further operations was to prove a crucial omission and to present logistical uncertainty for the remainder of 1943.[145]

The next time the Allies sat together to discuss the Mediterranean campaign was at the Trident conference in Washington from 12 to 25 May 1943. A memorandum was issued by Eisenhower, with the support of Cunningham and Tedder, to the CCS on 14 May at the outset of Husky discussions which concluded that the invasion of Sardinia and Corsica rather than mainland Italy should be the next objective.[146] Churchill contested this advice and the Allies could not agree a way forward. Frustrated that no plan had been agreed for an invasion of mainland Italy, and on the basis that Eisenhower had been invested with the responsibility to decide on any action following the invasion of Sicily, Churchill then flew with General Marshall from Washington to North Africa to attend what became known as the Algiers conference which convened on 29 May 1943. Churchill directed exhaustive talks which ended on 3 June and outlined what was essentially another Allied political compromise by summarising that 'post-Husky would be in General Eisenhower's hands and that he would recommend to the Combined Chiefs of Staff whichever operation seemed best'.[147]

Eisenhower had outlined three possibilities: 1) if the enemy collapsed quickly in Sicily, immediate operations would be undertaken against the Italian mainland; 2) if the enemy offered prolonged resistance in Sicily, no Allied resources would be available for immediate post-Sicily operations; and 3) if resistance was stubborn but could be overcome by mid-August, no decision would be made in advance.[148] Eisenhower agreed he would designate two separate headquarters to plan for the alternative courses of action. With just thirty-seven days to go to D-day, this tentativeness and lack of operational certainty would further challenge those charged with campaign maintenance and administration. The logisticians had to now make allowances for a whole range of possible post-Husky maintenance outcomes at this very late stage in their preparations for the invasion of Sicily.

Conclusions

The cumulative impact of the logistical challenges generated by the tortuous planning process created a monumental task for those charged with the responsibility of administering and maintaining Operation Husky. A deeply flawed preliminary plan with no logistical anchoring or post-action objectives was issued as a basis for the administration of the campaign. The highly complex planning and operational command structure that was established was, in hindsight, structurally unsound and these challenges were compounded by the distraction of the Tunisian war which occupied all the principal Husky commanders for three and a half months of the five month Husky planning period. The lack of one senior commander, totally and exclusively focused on invasion preparations, was keenly felt throughout this period. The late introduction of the UK-based Canadian forces in place of the British 3rd Division in the Husky battle order, while politically expedient, caused additional headaches for the logisticians both in London and in the Mediterranean. A miscalculation in the JPS plan with respect to the shipping needs of Husky, coupled with a shortage in the availability of specialised invasion craft threatened the Sicilian invasion in April 1943. Ultimately, the Allies decided to delay the possibility of a Normandy operation into 1944 in order to free up the necessary shipping capacity for Husky. This confluence of a flawed initial plan, the distractions of the Tunisian war, organisational misalignments and a vacuum of leadership, exacerbated by the distances between headquarters, resulted in a protracted planning process with the plan undergoing seven significant iterations. Unnecessary tensions arose as a result and the period was marked by inter-service and inter-Allied friction.

And yet, as will be discussed in the next chapter, the logisticians were able to cope with the many changes wrought by the tortuous planning process and their operational commanders by the creation a series of administrative orders from mid-February onwards. These plans were bedded into a flexible framework with degrees of freedom and inbuilt safety margins which could absorb the shocks of frequent planning changes

Chapter Three
Filling the Leadership Void

As already discussed, the logisticians faced immense challenges as they prepared the army and its naval armada for the British ETF landings on 10 July 1943. An immediate priority was to quickly to get to grips with the less than perfect command structure that had been gifted to them from on high. There were so many different units that were engaged in Operation Husky - Force 141, Force 545, GHQ ME, AFHQ as well as the War Office in London and Washington. An operational framework would need to be created with clarity and distinction as to roles and responsibilities, and with lines of demarcation clearly delineated. The complex logistics associated with troop movements, loading schedules and embarkation plans would then have to be addressed. There was also a pressing requirement for combined operations training in advance of the invasion. And the fresh operational assault intelligence, which emerged from the two most recent amphibious assaults, Operation Torch in November 1942 and Operation Corkscrew in June 1943, would need to be recycled back into the Husky invasion protocols. Procedures for beach maintenance which had proved to be inadequate for Operation Torch needed to evolve in order to supply assault forces across the beaches. And the hazardous work required to map, select and identify the assault beaches on southeastern Sicily urgently needed to begin. There was so much to do and so little time in which to do it.

Operation Husky Logistics Structure

As stated in Chapter One, Force 141 had responsibility for outline planning of Operation Husky as well as the coordination of the detailed planning for the campaign, but it had no executive responsibility for the administration or maintenance of the task force. The more detailed operational planning for Husky was the responsibility of the ETF itself and Force 545 was created on 22 February to manage the British combined naval and ground force logistics of the campaign.[149] The staff of Force 545 were inter-service but all British and were led by Admiral Ramsay and Lieutenant General M. C. Dempsey, who would both have operational roles in the invasion: Ramsay would be responsible for the ETF naval armada; Dempsey would be the commander of XIII Corps, one of the two Corps that would make up the ETF. Dempsey worked as Chief of Staff of Force 545 until the arrival of Major-General F. de Guingand from Eighth Army on 15 April when Dempsey rejoined XIII Corps. Coordinating all logistics for Force 545 was Brigadier M. W. Graham, the Deputy Adjutant and Quarter Master General (DA & QMG) from Montgomery's Eighth Army. The make-up of Force 545 was much better structured than Force 141, incorporating operational as well as logistics officers under one organisational roof. The interplay between this team, Force 141, GHQ ME and the AFHQ CAO function was to prove critical in ensuring the administrative preparations for the invasion proceeded despite the planning mess. To facilitate closer coordination of the embarkation and the maintenance of the ETF, Force 545 subsequently moved to Cairo on 19 April to be in close proximity to GHQ MEF.

Force 141's head Gairdner had two direct reports underneath him: the British Brigadier W. H. A. Bishop; and the American Brigadier-General Archelaus Hamblen with British staff representing Q (Maintenance), Q (Movements and Transportation), A Branch and the equivalent American staff from G-1 and G-4 branches.[150] At the end of March, Bishop was replaced by the vastly experienced Brigadier E. P. Nares who had been DA & QMG of the Western Desert Force.[151] Graham, Nares and Gale had absolutely pivotal roles in the British logistical preparations ahead of the invasion of Sicily.

The structure for administering Operation Husky was more logical and practical than that conceived for the actual planning of the campaign. It was decided that the authority which was geographically closest to the relevant British army and naval force would be given the responsibility for its initial administration, that is assault loading and initial beach maintenance. So, for instance, GHQ ME in Cairo was responsible for British forces assembling in the Middle East, AFHQ in Algiers responsible for British forces assembling in North Africa, and the War Office in London responsible for the Canadian forces assembling in the United Kingdom.[152] Extensive and well-run Allied logistics bases had already been established under GHQ ME and under AFHQ for the North African campaign. Force 545 had the responsibility of making its own administrative plan while coordinating all invasion preparations with GHQ ME, AFHQ and the War Office in London. The administration structure for Husky was not simple but the most important advantage in favour of the British forces was that they had been operating together successfully in North Africa since June 1940. This had been a campaign that was particularly challenging from a logistics perspective, where distances were enormous and where lines of supply were regularly stretched. Logisticians from all the supporting services had gained invaluable experience working together and appreciated the value of close coordination. The official British historian tells us that:

> the campaigns in Africa had bred a race of administrative officers and men in staffs and administrative units and services who had thoroughly learned how to conduct their hard business in the uncertain circumstances of war.[153]

As already chronicled, the operational plan was in a state of flux until early May but this ability to bring logistical clarity and foresight to uncertain situations is best exemplified by the AFHQ CAO in a memorandum penned on 25 February 1943.[154] Gale would only have been aware of the Operation Husky plans from early February but he demonstrates an ability, even at this early stage, to accurately predict the possible post-Husky outcomes and propose the most efficient administration and maintenance imperatives in order that supply depots and LofC could be most conveniently located:

> If British forces are to remain indefinitely in Sicily

they should be given their own base - with their own reserves - in the Island itself. This will avoid transshipment and therefore double-handling.

That the original administrative plans for Operation Husky saw so few changes from first draft in February through to the invasion in July, is testimony to the exceptional foresight, competence and capability of individuals such as Gale.

The Operation Husky logistics operation can best be divided into four broad phases;

1.   Preparation of the invasion up to embarkation,
2.   The phase covering the voyage and assault until Army HQs were established ashore,
3.   The further development of the operation according to the plan to reduce the island,
4.   A long-term future which might include an advance across the sea to the Italian mainland.

Force 545 would be broadly responsible for phases one and two. In phase three, HQ Fifteenth Army Group would assume administrative control for the coordination of all ground and air forces in Sicily. During this phase, the ETF would have its own bases and axis of supply on the island, with GHQ MEF responsible for their maintenance. It would be responsible for its own local administration by the standard British system of Lines of Communication Areas (LofC Area) and Sub-Areas.[155] The general administration of ports and beaches in eastern Sicily would be the ultimate responsibility of an organisation called Fortbase which will be discussed in the next chapter. Finally, during the fourth phase, the ETF and WTF's separate bases and axes of supply would merge into consolidated bases, with common axes of supply from North African ports and from outside the Mediterranean. AFHQ would then assume full administrative responsibility for the Mediterranean theatre and GHQ MEF would fade out of the picture.

Maintenance and Administration Plans of Force 141 and Force 545

Operation Husky was governed by a series of high-level planning instructions, administrative and maintenance outline appreciation projects and, finally, operational instructions which were issued between 12 February 1943 right up to the end of the campaign on 17 August. HQ Force 141 issued Planning Instruction No. 1 on 12 February which was to iterate many times in the following weeks as was discussed in Chapter One. However, it was the three Administrative Appreciation and Outline Maintenance Projects, issued by HQ Force 141 on 9 March, 23 March and 15 April, which were to govern the overall logistics of the campaign. It will not be possible to analyse each of the three projects, but the third project will be examined in some detail. The rationale for a second outline project so soon after the first one was stated as follows:

> In view of the urgency of establishing a basis for Administrative planning for Husky, this 2nd project has been prepared before the operational plan has been completed. It has been based on the operational outline plan, as it stands at the date of issue of this project.[156]

This was a clear indication that the logisticians had already anticipated that final operational plans would be in a state of flux for some time and that there was a need to provide a spine of administrative certainty for the invasion preparations as soon as possible.

The Third Outline Maintenance Project was issued by Nares on 15 April and, with sixty-eight separate logistics sections, it was a remarkably detailed document, especially given that Force 141 had only been begun detailed planning on 12 February, less than eight weeks earlier.[157] The 'Bigot - Husky' project began with a statement of very clear principles regarding maintenance protocols. It precisely defined the responsibilities of Force 141 and the ETF/WTF on the one hand, and the ETF/WTF and its support and supply chains on the other, which has already been detailed earlier in this chapter.[158] The Reserves Policy was outlined and it was ordained that each assault convoy must land sufficient maintenance to cover the needs of the troops ashore until the arrival of the next convoy, estimated to be between D+5 and D+7, building up gradually to a target state of thirty days reserve plus ten days working margin. It was decided that the control of base areas - store and supply depots - would be the responsibility of the ETF until such time as Fifteenth Army Group HQ could get established on the island and relieve Force 545 of this commitment. A provisional convoy programme was also set out but, as the operational plan was so drastically altered in May, this is of limited historical importance and the convoy programme will rather be examined at the task force level later in this section when Force 545's administrative plans are scrutinised. Detailed analysis of Sicilian port capacities was provided, not just for the major ports, but also for minor ports, harbours and even jetties. Details of the embarkation points in the Mediterranean and the location of the assault beaches for each division were listed, together with the projected maintenance capacities of each beach. The capacities of ships and craft were provided to enable the planning of load schedules, and assaulting units were instructed to land with Assault Scales of transport, moving up to Light Scales on the arrival of the first follow-up convoys.[159] Daily anticipated expenditure rates of the following were provided: all types of ammunition and ordinance, petrol, oil and lubricants (POL), water and aviation spirit.[160] There were sections covering the clothing policy for troops, gas equipment, mountain equipment, pack transport, and the waterproofing of vehicles. Prioritised work schedules were distributed to the Royal Engineers, with beach development and the repair of ports and airfields at the top of the list. Finally, the provision of the essential civilian needs of the Sicilian population had been calculated with, for instance, deliveries of coal and oil scheduled to arrive from D+5 to D+42. An outline plan for the governance of Sicily, post reduction, was issued separately when the Allied Military Government for Occupied Territories (AMGOT) would assume responsibility for civil affairs on the island. The information in all these documents was remarkably precise and detailed, especially given all the planning uncertainty during that period, and it demonstrates how the logisticians simply moved ahead with the business of invasion preparation in a smooth and coordinated fashion.

Just thirteen days later, and only nine days since the relocation of Force 545 to Cairo, Graham issued Twelfth Army Administrative Planning Instruction No. 1. Force 141's maintenance project had been issued to the entire invasion force, while this instruction was solely for the purposes of the ETF. It provided sufficient information to enable XIII and XXX Corps, the two formations making up the ETF, in turn to make their own administrative plans.[161] It did not deal with the pre-embarkation movements of troops, equipment, vehicles or stores as this responsibility fell to GHQ ME for XIII Corps, and to AFHQ for XXX Corps, and those movements were the subject of separate orders. However, convoy tables with a provisional allotment of shipping were included in the instruction as detailed at Appendix B, with each ship assigned to a particular beach. XIII and XXX Corps were then responsible for completing a series of documents, by 17 and 19 May respectively, which detailed the complete contents of the ships which would transport them to Sicily. This was to include the allocation decisions they were to make to ensure the right troops and equipment were loaded in the right craft, aimed at the correct beach and would tactically unload in the sequence required for immediate combat activities.[162] The availability of onshore transport had emerged as a critical problem at this juncture and it was decided that all first, second and third line transport must be organised on a pooled basis for any load-carrying tasks that might arise. Traffic control was highlighted as another major problem to be faced and, with troop movements and maintenance convoys running in conflicting directions, both XIII and XXX Corps were tasked with drawing up traffic plans.

The Force 545 instruction was more demanding from a maintenance perspective than the Force 141 version, particularly with respect to the period by which formations should be brought from assault scales up to light scales. Graham wanted the ETF on light scales by the D+3 convoy but, owing to limited shipping space, some formations would be without any second line transport on D+3 and others with only a portion of it.[163] Rations for consumption during the voyage would be provided on all ships and each soldier was to be issued with a forty-eight hour mess tin ration which was solely for consumption after disembarkation. Rations for D+2 and beyond would be drawn by each soldier's unit from the supply depot.[164] Tentage and anti-mosquito protection was specified with anti-mosquito veils issued to every soldier. Each tent was to be equipped with sand-fly proof bush nets, while each unit was instructed to draw eighteen and a half pounds of anti-mosquito cream and one and a half gallons of Flysol for every hundred men, prior to embarkation. The level of minute detail inherent in these instructions is demonstrated at Appendix C, where the anti-malarial manifest is set out. Waterproofing of vehicles and equipment, and their subsequent de-waterproofing after disembarkation, was viewed as a most important subject and Corps commanders were warned that the whole amphibious invasion might be jeopardised if procedures weren't followed:

> The success of any combined operation involving the landing of AFVs and MT depends largely on the ability of such vehicles to withstand immersion in sea water and function immediately afterwards[165]…Although the process of waterproofing must not be regarded as complicated or highly technical, a very close study must be made by every officer and man concerned of measures to be adopted and their implications. Organisation within the unit must be highly developed however to ensure that no vehicle or piece of equipment is put out of action.[166]

On 19 May, Graham issued Twelfth Army Administrative Planning Instruction No. 2 with the objective of clarifying how the administrative situation in Sicily would be managed between D-day and the establishment of Fifteenth Army Group on the island. This was estimated not to happen until at least D+14, and HQ XIII Corps together with its administrative function, HQ 86 Area, was assigned the task of bridging the maintenance gap for the ETF.[167] The administration responsibility for the ETF was agreed as follows: recce parties from HQ 86 Area would accompany the assault convoy, with the main body landing on the D+3 convoy; once Syracuse was captured, HQ 86 Area would assume control of that port; HQ 151 Sub-Area would assume control for Augusta when it was captured, but under the command of HQ 86 Area; when Catania was captured, a Sub-Area from the United Kingdom would take over Syracuse, with HQ 86 Area assuming control for Catania; HQ 86 Area would maintain supervision of all Sub-Areas and all captured ports in eastern Sicily.[168]

During May and June, HQ XXX Corps and HQ XIII Corps in turn issued a series of administrative instructions which were the detailed application of the Force 141 and Force 545 directives. The Corps administrative staff had to deal not only with the widely dispersed HQ network, but also with the challenge that their own formations were located in many places. For instance, XIII Corps HQ had to deal with four separate HQs just for the mounting of 51st Highland Division: Force 545 (1,500 miles away), Force 141 (500 miles away), AFHQ (500 miles away) and Tripoli Base HQ (350 miles away) while 51st Highland division itself was located 350 miles away from HQ XXX Corps.[169] HQ XIII Corps was arguably more challenged with formations scattered over fifteen different locations on 4 May - Cairo, Beni Yusef, Damascus, Tripoli, Tobruch, Qatana, Aartouz, Paiforce, Kabrit, Mena, Rafa, Qassassin, Palestine, Nuseirat and Gaza.[170]

Embarkation Logistics for XIII Corps

As early as the end of February 1943, GHQ ME had estimated that, in order to mount approximately 46,500 men of XIII Corps from the Middle East for the D-day assault, it would require the loading of sixty MT/Stores ships, twenty-five troop ships and a large number of landing craft.[171] An earlier constraint, that of the availability of adequate shipping for transporting the amphibious invasion, had now been supplanted by a concern about how quickly supply ships could be offloaded at the assault beaches. Not only were off-loading craft in short supply, but so were qualified stevedores and, as the final plan targeted much narrower frontal assaults than was originally contemplated, there simply would not be enough room on the beaches to offload and expedite the volume of materiel that was required. It was decided, therefore, that there was only sufficient capacity to work fifteen ships at a time at the designated beaches so GHQ ME divided the supply convoys into two thirty ship fleets, one landing on D-day and the second on D+3. In order to get MTs and supplies onshore as quickly as possible, each convoy was further subdivided into two categories, 15A and 15B ships. So, on D-day, the contents of fifteen category A ships would be disgorged onto the beach by sixty-five stevedores stationed on board each vessel. Later that morning, the category A ships would depart the shore to be replaced by fifteen category B ships and the same stevedores would join a pre-determined category B ship and began offloading it. The whole process would be repeated on D+3 by the same stevedores who had stayed on the beaches for the intervening three days and, in the meantime, had helped establish the supply depots.[172] In this way, logisticians attempted to create the most efficient logistical framework possible when set against the various operational constraints they faced. The splitting of the convoys into two separate D-day and D+3 fleets explained why both the Third Outline Maintenance Project and the Twelfth Army Administrative Planning Instruction No. 2 contained first and second line transport caveats.

Each convoy ship had to be completely loaded and ready to sail by D-7. Store ships were to be tactically stowed in the order that vehicles and supplies would be discharged onto the assault beaches and in the order of priority set out in Loading Tables which had been prepared by Force 545. From the middle of April, a pre-stowage planning staff was set up at GHQ ME to help manage these procedures. Landing tables for XIII Corps were received from Force 545 on 22 May when detailed planning of vehicles and stores stowage for each ship could commence. The total lift was finally fixed at 12,350 tons of supplies, 3,558 vehicles for D-day and 47,761 tons of supplies and 4,367 vehicles for D+3.[173]

Once the shipping plan had been established for XIII Corps, the focus of the logisticians moved to the complex task of moving assault personnel and stores from their many locations across the Mediterranean to the principal embarkation ports of Benghazi, Suez, Haifa, Beirut and Alexandria. This was done by road, by rail and by sea and, during June, 65,693 troops, 9,442 vehicles and 60,111 tons of stores were moved to these ports.[174] While it would have been more efficient to transport these payloads by sea, the vast majority of vessels needed to be stationed in port and prepared for D-day. In the end, 56,775 troops with 8,740 vehicles endured lengthy and complicated rail and road journeys to reach their assigned embarkation ports. The detail of all the pre-embarkation movements and the composition and contents of the D-day and D+3 convoys for XIII Corps are set out at Appendix D.

Training

Overlaid on top of the planning and execution of the main movement programmes, was the need to provide the assault troops with training in amphibious warfare and, most critically, provide the officers running the beach groups with the practices and competencies needed to maintain an army over beaches for an extended period of time. Training was a particularly high priority for the army and naval forces of the ETF as they had virtually no experience of combined operations, amphibious assaults or prolonged beach maintenance. A British Combined Training Centre (CTC) was established at Djedjelli in Algeria and was expected to be functioning on 1 May. Following numerous delays caused by the later than anticipated ending of the Tunisian war, with the identification of training personnel, and in the sourcing of assault equipment, the CTC was only ready to begin training programmes on 15 May.[175]

All the senior Husky commanders demonstrated their concerns that inadequate combined operations training ahead of the invasion might jeopardise the prospects of a successful invasion. Montgomery in particular was acutely aware of this need and, as early as 19 April, he wrote to the CIGS saying that:

> the Divisions now fighting with me who are to take part in Husky, must all be withdrawn from the present operations in Tunisia fairly soon. If this is not done, then Husky may well fail. That would be frightful.[176]

On 5 May, with the Tunisian war still not finished, he again writes to the CIGS: 'I am now pulling 51 Div into reserve as it must start special training.'[177] So much needed to be achieved in a such a very short space of time and various pieces of new equipment needed to be tested even before training could began.[178] Establishing a bridge between the various types of assault craft and the Sicilian shore had occupied the minds of logisticians for some time. Both Naval Pontoons and Treadway Bridging were tested at CTC in an effort to bridge the gap between, in particular, Landing Ship Tanks (LSTs) weighing 2,000 tons, and the shore.[179] It transpired that Treadway Bridging was unsatisfactory for this purpose and it was discarded as a reliable bridging solution while Naval Pontoons were adopted, with responsibility for handling this equipment being given to the Navy. In addition, there were courses in how to handle, stow and erect Bailey Bridges, a portable pre-fabricated truss bridge, and all mine-sweeping craft officers attended the Mine Warfare school. Given the topography in Sicily, lessons in Mountain Warfare were offered with a team available to demonstrate the uses of mountain warfare equipment, which unfortunately arrived too late in the theatre for widespread distribution. It is clear that the Husky commanders were very focused on training their armies to fight on a very different battlefield than that of North Africa.

On 13 March, Eisenhower requested that every effort was to be made by the War Office to provide mountain warfare training in addition to amphibious training for formations assembling in the UK.[180] More traditional forms of transportation would also be central to the Husky supply chain. Authority was given to local formation commanders in North Africa to acquire donkeys and mules in any reasonable scale, with personnel from Pack Transport Convoys available within reach of units to assist in training. The DUKW, a two and a half ton amphibian vehicle manufactured by General Motors Corporation in the United States, was to be used for the first time and much expectation was riding on their ability to answer the problem of maintenance over the beaches.[181] As they would be required to work for twenty-four hours a day, it was estimated that each DUKW would require one driver and one boat hook man working together in eight to ten hour shifts. Small groups of British vehicle instructors were flown to Arzew in Algeria for a course of instruction in DUKWs at the United States training school, before being flown to CTC and to Sousse to train the DUKW drivers. The ETF would have 350 DUKWs on D-day for use by beach maintenance crews and 125 men would be trained as drivers at the CTC as well as 750 men at Sousse, which was closer to where the beach group were forming up, during a three week intensive course which included basic instruction in seamanship.[182]

When it comes to larger scale combined operations rehearsals, a significant portion of the British forces mounted from the Middle East were limited to less than satisfactory 'dryshod' training in the desert, that is exercises carried out on land that attempted to simulate landings from sea craft. Despite their shortage of preparation time, the 1st Canadian Infantry Division had some useful training in Scotland before they left for the Mediterranean and their final and most important assault exercise was planned for 17-20 June on a section of the Ayrshire coast in the vicinity of Troon which was selected as the local topography resembled that of the Pachino peninsula, their Sicilian destination. Exercise Stymie, which was to be 'one of the greatest full scale combined operations manoeuvres yet held in the British Isles', had to be cancelled soon after it started, owing to high winds which made the seas too dangerous for the landing craft.[183] One of the largest amphibious rehearsals in the Middle East took place from 10 June onwards when 151 Brigade (50th Division) and 15 and 17 Brigades (5th Division) of XIII Corps, totaling 23,037 troops of all ranks on twelve personnel ships and with 344 vehicles on four MT ships, embarked from Suez. The four MT ships were stowed with non-operational vehicles as well as dummy stores and the exercise, which involved troop, vehicle and store disembarkation by landing craft at beaches near Suez, was completed on 19 June when the brigades returned to their original locations in the troop assembly areas.[184] It was unfortunate that owing to operational commitments, the Air Forces were unable to offer more than a token level of cooperation and, in his despatch, Alexander describes this exercise as 'some very incomplete landing rehearsals in the Gulf of Aqaba'.[185]

A report produced for Fifteenth Army Group on 12 July 1943, outlining the lessons learned for future training programmes, highlights how challenging it was to train formations that were so far apart, in such a short space of time and when the availability of instructors and training equipment was so unreliable.[186] It was a race against time and as Alexander admitted in his dispatch, he was particularly concerned about both the quantity and quality of pre-invasion combined operations training and said it 'was not as thorough as I should have liked, but the pressing considerations of time and shortage of craft imposed serious limitations'.[187]

Lessons learned from Operation Torch and Operation Corkscrew

The Allied invasions of French North Africa (Operation Torch) in November 1942 and the invasion of the island of Pantelleria (Operation Corkscrew) in June 1943 afforded Operation Husky planners and logisticians some recent amphibious actions from which to garner intelligence, particularly in the area of assault craft disembarkation. Operation Torch was a complex three pronged amphibious assault involving 107,000 troops and 850 naval craft and was a rich source of combined operations learning. Some of this was helpful from a Husky perspective but some of it was not and actually contributed to the planning uncertainties which dogged the planning process up to May 1943. Although virtually unopposed, the Torch landings had highlighted a lack of specialised assault equipment as well as a dysfunctional beach group maintenance system, exacerbated by cohorts of poorly trained officers and men. Sir Bernard Fergusson, who was Director of Combined Operations from 1945 to 1946, said of Torch that 'any idea of prolonged maintenance over beaches was heretical, despite the experience of Gallipoli'.[188] Major General J. C. Haydon, Vice Chief of Combined Operations for Operation Torch, wrote a post action report entitled 'Impressions gained from the Assault Phase of the Operations in North Africa' in which he said that 'it appears doubtful whether any assault plan should rely for more than twenty-four hours continuous maintenance over unsheltered beaches'.[189] This view was accepted as doctrinally accurate by the JPS planners and led to the belief that the rapid capture of ports and airfields in Sicily would be essential in order to maintain troops in the field.

Operation Corkscrew was arguably more valuable as a learning opportunity, given it was just four weeks before the Husky D-day but only if lessons learned could be quickly recycled back to the assault forces. The British 1st Infantry Division met no resistance when they landed on Pantelleria, but they had the opportunity to conduct an amphibious assault and assess its performance in a live fire exercise. Just two days after the island surrendered on 11 June, Colonel A. H. Head from Force 141 distributed a note with fifteen separate performance observations, three of which were critical to the forthcoming invasion of Sicily.[190] Head had been personally assigned from Combined Operations HQ in London to Force 141 by Lord Louis Mountbatten, who was then the Director of British Combined Operations, and so he had a keen sense of what was required for a successful amphibious assault.[191] First, while the performance of the Landing Craft Infantry (LCI) which transported troops to just off their destination was excellent, he observed that the LCAs (Landing Craft Assault) which each carried thirty-five men to the beaches, spent far too long forming up alongside the LCIs before moving off, leaving them vulnerable to air attack as well as bombardment from coastal defences. Secondly, communications between the beach groups, the Senior Naval Officers Landing (SNOL) and the HQ ship did not work in the early stages of the landings with the result that that there was delay and confusion. Head additionally pointed out that these types of signals issues had also been observed during training at Djedjelli and could be a much more significant issue during the Husky assault, the early stages of which would take place in darkness. Finally, Head was concerned about lax security arrangements at embarkation ports which meant that 'many natives and unreliable locals and any second-rate spy could have gauged the date of sailing' of Operation Corkscrew.[192] Unless security was tightened up prior to the Husky embarkations, the critical element of assault surprise, which was highly coveted by the assault forces, would be lost. All of Head's observations were quickly passed through to task commanders and then down the ranks to individual units so that the lessons learned could be applied to Husky preparations. In fact, in his post-action despatch on the invasion of Sicily, Admiral Cunningham said the capturing of Pantelleria was 'accomplished without prejudice to Husky, of which operation indeed it was an essential preliminary'.[193]

Beach Bricks and Beach Groups

In his monthly report for January 1943, the Director of Staff

Duties (DSD) at the War Office stated that there was a need for a new organisation to maintain an assault force across beaches until such time as a port could be captured and got into working order.[194] One of the key findings from Operation Torch in November 1942 was the need for improved beach management and, in the eight months up to Operation Husky, significant developments led to an improved organisation called a Beach Brick.[195] The staffing of these units became contentious as, with manpower at a premium, locking men up in specialised units for one temporary operation was inefficient. Maitland-Wilson wrote to the CIGs on 3 July expressing his concerns that Eisenhower wanted to be able to break up such formations and use them as first assault reinforcements.[196] The DSD solution was to build Beach Groups around individual infantry battalions, reporting to the battalion HQ, the staff and men of which would revert to their primary duties once beach work had been completed. Additionally, Beach HQs were to be established as the LofC Sub-Area for a set of beaches, with several Beach Groups under their control. In this way, supply depots could be quickly established after the assault phase in a coordinated fashion, with continuity of ownership of the LofC, until Fifteenth Army Group HQ arrived on the island. The general duties of the Beach Groups were:

1.   To arrange and control the movement of all personnel and vehicles from ships and landing craft to assembly areas inland.

2.   To move stores, etc. from ships' holds and from landing craft to Beach Maintenance Area.

3.   To develop and organise beaches and the beach maintenance area for defence, movements and for administrative purposes, including evacuation of casualties and recovery of vehicles.

4.   To provide a three service Beach Signals organisation.[197]

A Beach Group consisted of up to 3,000 men of all ranks, with up to twenty different units and services working together.[198] Engineer, medical, artillery and signal detachments as well as naval Beach Masters and army landing officers were established around a nucleus of infantry and the ETF had eight separate Beach Groups as detailed in Figure 8.[199] Each Beach Group was assigned to an assault beach and allocated landing craft and DUKWs for store transportation purposes. Two LofC Sub-areas sat atop this logistics structure: 86 LofC Area (later 151 LofC Area) for XIII Corps and 103 LofC Sub-Area for XXX Corps. During April, May and June 1943, Beach Groups were assembled and trained together in the Middle East, North Africa and the United Kingdom and each had some subtle variations, as is detailed at Appendix E.

Distribution of Beach Groups and DUKWs

Formation	Beach	Beach Group	Infantry nucleus	Craft*	DUKW*	Co-ordinating Administrative H.Q.s
13th Corps: 5th Division	44	33	1st Argyll and Sutherland Highlanders	12 L.C.T.	45	86 L. of C. Area, later 151 L. of C. Area
	45 46	32	2nd H.L.I.	24 L.C.T	45	
50th Division	47	34	1st Welch Regt.		50	
30th Corps: 231st Brigade	51 52	31	7th Bn R. Marines	6 L.C.T.	9	103 L. of C. Sub-Area
51st Division	56	20 21	2/4th Hampshires	9 L.C.T.	105	
1st Canadian Division	57 (Closed D+3)	3 4	11, 188 and 242 Pioneer Coys. 73, 84 and 238 Pioneer Coys.	9 L.C.T.	96	

* The figures shown are as a general illustration only. Numbers fluctuated, and there is no exact record. Besides L.C.T., other craft, e.g. L.C.M. were used. However something like these numbers would have been at work on an 'average' day.

Figure 8
Distribution of Formations, Target Beaches, Beach Groups, Infantry Nucleus and Assault Craft [200]

Reconnaissance and Beach Selection

Although the ETF and WTF would ultimately land on two strips of beaches, each approximately fifty miles long at the southeastern tip of Sicily, the original JPS plan had envisaged multiple beach landings between Palermo and Syracuse. Preliminary reconnaissance had in fact been conducted for ninety-four beaches around the entire island and this information was given to Force 141 with the JPS plan in February 1943 – see Figure 9.

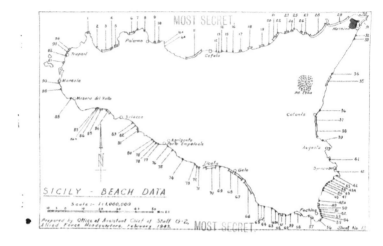

Figure 9
Sicily - Beach Data, February 1943 [201]

With the final Husky plan and, in turn the assault beaches, not confirmed until early May, it was necessary, therefore, to continue beach and beachhead reconnaissance over the 300-mile coastline between Syracuse and Palermo. Precise information on the nature of the coastline and its immediate hinterland, was essential in order that the chances of invasion and maintenance success could be optimised. Key determinants in the selection of the perfect beach included: the nature of the sea approaches to the beaches and whether underwater hazards such as rocks existed; the state and depth of the sea bottom as well as the gradient of the approach to land; and finally, whether the beach was sandy or stony. A key feature of Sicilian beaches is the presence of false beaches or sand bars between twenty-five and fifty meters offshore which provide limited clearance for craft. These would need to be reconnoitered, the likelihood of the grounding of landing craft estimated, and the best solution then agreed upon for landing troops and supplies over the water gap. This might take the form of pontoons if the water was deep or, if the water was shallow, troops could wade ashore and waterproofed vehicles drive straight up on to the beach. The nature of the exit inland from the beaches might then rule out a good landing beach if for instance the exit was blocked by cliffs, a regular feature of the Sicilian coastline. Reconnaissance was an ongoing process with new updates and refinements constantly being made. In fact, Gairdner warned formations on 18 March 1943, in Planning Instruction No. 7, Beach Intelligence Summaries, that 'further reconnaissance is being carried out and amendments to this document will be forwarded from time to time'.[202] Beach data was even being updated as the convoys sailed for Sicily. Major J. M. Robinson, Divisional Photo Interpreter, who had flown to Malta from England and then reconnoitered the Canadian target beaches at the Pachino peninsula from a submarine, was landed as late as 7 July by bosun's chair on HMS *Hilary* with last-minute beach intelligence for the Canadian formations onboard.[203]

The year 1943 was a significant one for innovation not only in amphibious assault equipment but also in reconnaissance techniques. This reconnaissance work was conducted in two novel ways, by aerial photography and by specialized beach reconnaissance parties. The Northwest African Photographic Reconnaissance Wing (NAPRW) was an Allied photographic reconnaissance wing, created at the Casablanca conference in January 1943, and 'which demonstrated the excellence of the camera as an instrument of war'.[204] NAPRW began surveying Sicilian airfields, ports, beaches and beach defences, industrial areas and the Axis LofC on a regular basis. Between 16 May and 9 July, they made 1086 reconnaissance sorties of Sicily from northwest Africa and from Malta. Molony reported that the war diaries of many army units contained copies of the photographs taken on these flights, showing that they were broadly distributed and widely appreciated.[205] While aerial photographs revealed a great deal, most of the facts had to be discovered at first hand and as early as 6 February beach reconnaissance parties began leaving the Middle East for Malta to begin their work.[206] Termed Combined Operations Pilotage Parties (COPP), small joint teams of officers and men of the Royal Navy and the Royal Engineers were launched at night from submarines close to the Sicilian shore either in chariots (a slow moving torpedo-like weapon operated by two divers sitting astride) or in collapsible canoes called folbots.[207] Water depth was measured by weighted lines, distance from shore by fishing line and core samples were taken back from every beach. This was extremely dangerous work and by the end of March 1943, eleven out of thirty-one operatives had been lost.[208] Cunningham paid tribute to them in his despatch:

> Much credit is due to the officers and men of the beach reconnaissance parties for their arduous and hazardous effort to obtain details of the beach gradients and sandbars. Credit is also due to the submarines of the 8th and 10th Flotillas which worked on beach reconnaissance in company with these parties. Their casualties in this operation were unfortunately heavy; apart from natural dislike of such losses, the possibility of capture always gives rise to anxiety on grounds of security.[209]

Initial surveys showed that only thirty-two main beaches could be listed as possible for amphibious assault purposes, and of these, only twenty-six were ultimately selected.[210] The photographs, these surveys and assorted other pieces of intelligence were used to create models and maps of the beaches which were invaluable for the assault troops.[211] The men of the ETF would be made very familiar with the various contours and characteristics of the beaches they were to assault well in advance of their embarkation but they would have no knowledge of their actual destination until they were proceeding on the final leg of their sea passage to Sicily.

Conclusions

The challenges that faced the logisticians as a result of the planning delays and disagreements were immense. Although the Operation Husky logistics structure was marginally less complex than the planning structure, it was the collective experience of the various logistics teams, hard won in the North African campaign over a number of years, which proved to be the single most important factor in ensuring that the campaign was able to proceed to the timetable that had been established in January 1943. In addition, Force 545 was structured in a far better way than Force 141 with a combination of operational and logistics officers working together. What was particularly impressive about the senior administrators was how they brought logistical coherence and structure to a planning situation that was plagued by uncertainty. The Maintenance and Administration Plans that they issued, and the progressive updates that followed, were the fixed anchor that the ETF and all its constituent units and formations could rely upon. Possibly the most complex task was the transportation and embarkation of XXX Corps, its troops, stores and vehicles, from across the Mediterranean and this exercise proceeded with metronomic reliability. Although pre-invasion training for the ETF was something of a mixed bag, the establishment of Beach Groups, the lessons learned from Operations Torch and Corkscrew, and the coastal and beachhead reconnaissance that was conducted, provided the ETF as it embarked for Sicily with confidence in its ability to achieve invasion and campaign success. A map detailing Axis dispositions in Sicily and the target landing areas of the ETF task force is shown in Figure 10.

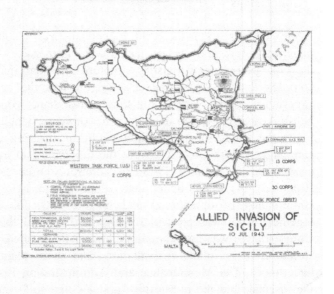

Figure 10
Axis dispositions in Sicily and the target landing areas of the ETF task force [212]

Chapter Four
The Invasion of Europe

Even the best prepared plans of logisticians and their battlefield commanders need to adapt to the reality of both the battlefield conditions and the battle itself. And this was manifestly to be the case with Operation Husky. Key beaches and landing sites proved to be more physically challenging than had been anticipated and were simply unable to support the disembarkation of materiel in the volumes necessary to support the advancing ETF. The convoys coming from the Clyde suffered at the hands of enemy U-boats which severely impacted the availability of First and Second Line of Transport vehicles. And to compound these challenges further, front line troops moved far quicker than had been expected and supply lines were dangerously stretched in the first seven days of the campaign. The logisticians would need to demonstrate flexibility and resourcefulness in order to adapt their plans to cope with these unexpected challenges and to achieve their goal of quickly establishing a stable LoC on the island.

Maintenance over the Bark West Beaches on D-day

Given the magnitude and scale of the invasion exercise - the full order of battle is detailed at Appendix F - this study will narrow its focus from the overall maintenance performance of the ETF to an analysis of how maintenance evolved for one division during the Sicilian campaign. The 1st Canadian Infantry Division, part of XXX Corps, was arguably set the greatest assault and maintenance challenges of all the divisions in the ETF: they had to cope with significant logistical challenges in preparing for a battle in a far distance operational theatre; troops disembarked straight onto beaches after two weeks at sea; the supply convoy suffered a grave setback whilst en route to Sicily; the assault beaches assigned to them proved to be the most challenging of all of the beaches targeted by the ETF because of their particular features as well as their orientation; and, finally, the Canadians carried out the longest and most rapid advance of all formations of the ETF in

Sicily and its maintenance during that period stretched the fledgling supply lines.[213]

An additional factor which drove the selection of this division is that the Canadian archives which focus on Operation Husky are extremely complete when it comes to material relating to the maintenance of the armies in the field, unlike the British equivalents which are less organised with significant gaps at times. This was made possible because 1st Canadian Infantry Division had an historical officer attached to it throughout the campaign.[214] Captain Sesia, who was previously an intelligence officer in the 1 Canadian Infantry Brigade, was charged with the task of collecting narratives of participants in Operation Husky, ensuring the preservation of all the documents and keeping a diary of his own observations.[215]

As has been detailed in Chapter One, the involvement of the Canadians in Operation Husky, then located in the United Kingdom, was only confirmed on 27 April, leaving them just seventy-four days to prepare for an assault on a foreign shore over 2370 miles away which was a monumental logistical feat.[216] The convoy coming from the United Kingdom, designated Force 'V', was commanded by Rear Admiral P. L. Vian and travelled in an unbroken voyage from the Clyde in Scotland to the western side of the Pachino peninsula. The logisticians divided the fleet into two separate convoys: a fast assault convoy termed KMF18 which was scheduled to land on D-day and which departed the Clyde on 28 June; and a slow supplies convoy termed KMF19 which was scheduled to land on D+3 and which departed between 19 and 24 June.[217] KMF18 contained the assault troops of the 1st Canadian Infantry Division, twelve Canadian tanks, as well as Nos. 3 and 4 Beach Groups. KMS19 contained the 1 Canadian Tank Brigade and a significant cargo of equipment, vehicles and troop rations. KMF18 was assault-loaded in the United Kingdom and, together with KMS19, had twenty-four days initial maintenance and ten days reserve on board. The actual loadings were: KMF18 D-day assault convoy, 4,750 tons; KMS19 D+3 convoy, 24,800 tons.[218] A total of 1,851 officers and 24,835 junior ranks were transported for Operation Husky in these two convoys.[219]

KMF18 had an uneventful trip to its release points off the Sicilian coast but, unfortunately, KMS19 was attacked on the night of 4 and 5 July by U-boats off the North African coast, between Oran and Algiers. Three ships were torpedoed and sunk: the SS's *City of Venice*, *St. Essylt* and the *Devis* which was the Commodore's ship.[220] These ships between them carried 470 Canadian troops, of whom one officer and fifty-four other ranks were reported missing, but over 562 vehicles were also lost including ninety-nine three ton trucks, one hundred and two fifteen hundred weight trucks and thirty-seven heavy utility vehicles.[221] The loss of all this transport and equipment was to create considerable maintenance challenges later as the Canadian divisional HQ lost most of its Second Line of Transport vehicles, rations for D+2 and beyond, and the majority of its signal equipment. Alternative transport arrangements were quickly put in place for the Canadian survivors, especially the essential stevedores of No. 1 Docks Group and 1007 and 1021 Docks Operating Companys. They were taken by a back-up destroyer to Bougie in Algeria where they were partially re-equipped and then sent on to Sicily, landing late on D+3.[222] The gaps created by the loss of supplies from the three ships in KMS19 were ultimately filled by later convoys but these wouldn't arrive until D+14 from the Middle East, with the first maintenance convoy from the United Kingdom scheduled for D+46. This left the logisticians with an immediate equipment and skill set shortage which they would need to contend with.

1st Canadian Infantry Division formed the left wing of the ETF and Force 'V' sailed them to the Release Positions on the west side of the Pachino peninsula, in the Bark West assault area on Beach 57.[223] This stretch of coastline had a total front of roughly 8,300 yards and was actually two beaches, designated Roger and Sugar, each of which was further subdivided into three zones: Red, Amber and Green as depicted in Figure 11.

LANDING OF I CDN INF DIV ON PACHINO PENINSULA
10 JUL 1943

Figure 11
**Landing of 1st Canadian Infantry Division, Pachino
Peninsula
10 July 1943** [224]

Pre-invasion reconnaissance had indicated that Beach 57
might be the most difficult of all the ETF assault beaches and
that it might be necessary to pass at least part of the Canadian
maintenance through Beach 56.[225] Although Beach 57 had
both Nos. 3 and 4 Beach Groups assigned to it, it was decided
at a very late stage to keep No. 4 Beach Group as a reserve
except for a small part of the group which was to land the 2
Canadian Infantry Brigade and its equipment on Roger beach.[226]
Fears about Beach 57 proved well founded. It had numerous
false beaches and fifty-five per cent of the LCMs carrying
troops on D-day, as well as forty per cent of the LCMs
carrying supplies on D+1, were stranded on these sandbars.[227]
This situation might have been at lot worse if a decision hadn't

been taken by the Divisional Commander and his logisticians to disembark the 1 Canadian Infantry Brigade into LCTs at the Release Position and then offload them again onto DUKWs just before they reached the sandbars, rather than running them straight onto the beach with LCAs. This order was only issued on 7 July and meant that certain troops had to make two transfers in heavy seas resulting in a key part of the assault, whose first phase objective was the capture of Pachino airfield, landing one hour and forty-four minutes late.[228] This caused considerable confusion among other ships in the assault convoy and in fact some personnel of No. 3 Beach Group arrived on Beach 57 before the assault troops.[229]

The weather provided another logistical challenge for the Beach Groups for, although the wind strength moderated from midnight onwards, the swell remained high and the westerly orientation of Beach 57 meant it was far more exposed to the prevailing elements than any other beach used by the ETF.[230] The logistical situation was quickly stabilised, however, when two reconnaissance exercises were conducted: first, naval officers sought and found a location that would be suitable for LSTs to land at the point of Grotticelle midway between Roger and Sugar beaches and, by 1100hrs, tanks and other vehicles were coming ashore dryshod; and secondly, a search was made by logisticians for a maintenance area which had to be conducted on foot by the Beach commander as his designated transportation was at the bottom of the Mediterranean.[231] It transpired that Beach 57, as well as being very narrow, had no natural exit points for mechanised transport, a key fault of the pre-invasion reconnaissance. However, 102 Field Company of the Royal Engineers quickly constructed a roadway of Sommerfeld Tracking 500 yards long and running inland to a lateral road.[232] Landing stores over Bark West continued to be a problem during D+1 owing to the false beaches but the DUKWs proved their worth by shuttling stores directly from the supply ships to the maintenance depot, a sketch of which is shown in Figure 12. Without these amphibious marvels, it is debatable whether the 1st Canadian Infantry Division, or for that matter the entire

ETF, could have been supplied over beaches as successfully as it was, given the challenges they faced. In August 1943, a War Office 'Report on Beach Maintenance – Sicily' noted that 'The DUKW is a magnificent bird and proved itself, in combined operations, the greatest invention of modern times'.[233]

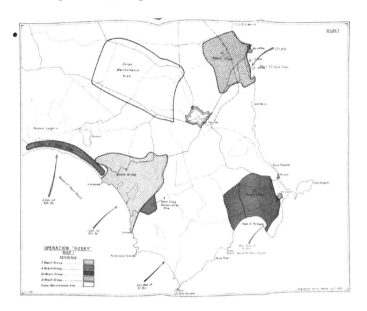

Figure 12
Maintenance of 1st Canadian Infantry Division at Pachino Peninsula over Beaches 56 and 57 on D-day [234]

Once the assault troops were safely ashore, the various administrative functions of the ETF began to come ashore in order to establish the necessary supply lines. 103 LofC Sub-Area landed on Roger beach at 1500hrs, No. 4 Beach Group at 1630hrs and an advance party from HQ XXX Corps at 1800hrs. By the evening of D-day, all the maintenance capability required to organise and supply the needs of the 1st Canadian Infantry Division were ashore.[235]

Establishing the Supply Lines

It became apparent that the maintenance of the 1st Canadian Infantry Division over Beach 57 was not going to be a sustainable option for stores discharge in the long term. On D+3 the logisticians made the decision to shut it down and to reassign No. 4 Beach Group to Beach 56 in the Bark South sector where it would begin priming the needs of the Canadian supply chain from that beach. No. 20 Beach Group, originally assigned to the 51st Highland Division, had been active at this location since D-Day but, in a process referred to as 'side-stepping', moved to Beach 52 from D+4 onwards.[236] No. 4 Beach Group took over the running of this entire beach, reinforced by No. 3 Beach Group which side-stepped from Beach 57 with additional support from 700 prisoners of war.[237] This arrangement proved highly successful and tonnage discharged grew from 1,104 tons on D+4 to 4,376 tons on D+11 and proved to be one of the most successful beach arrangements in Operation Husky.[238]

Italian resistance was far weaker than anticipated across the Bark beaches and, with events moving quicker than original plans had anticipated, the maintenance plan needed to alter so that supply lines could cope with the unforeseen demands. 103 LofC Sub-Area had originally been designated to supervise all of the XXX Corps Beach Groups. No sooner was it set up on D+6 at Pachino, however, than its supervisory duties were made surplus to requirement owing to the pace at which events were unfolding and, when HQ Eighth Army took control of all XXX Corps maintenance on D+7, it found itself relegated to an ordinary sub-area managing the supply depot at Pachino. The positions of the supply depots for maintaining XXX Corps had now moved by D+7 to that depicted in Figure 13.

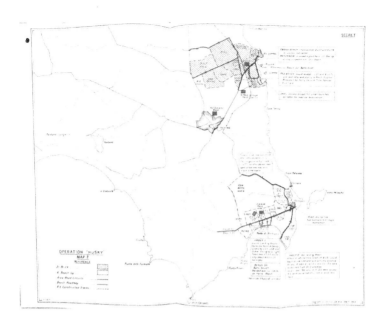

Figure 13
**Maintenance of XXX Corps at Pachino Peninsula over
Bark Beaches at D+7 [239]**

On D+10, the Bark sector beach groups started disbanding. No. 31 Beach Group, which had managed the Bark East sector, was 'sidestepped' north on 16 July to support the advance of XXX Corps to the east of Mount Etna while on 27 July No. 4 Beach Group left Sicily for Sousse followed by No. 3 Beach Group to Tripoli on 31 July. As the ports of Syracuse, Augusta and Catania came under ETF control, beach landings tailed off but the collective efforts of these units had resulted in the safe landing and discharge, over the Bark beaches alone, of more than 38,000 tons of stores, 4,000 vehicles and 32,000 men in just 14 days. This was an achievement that was materially greater than had been hoped for.[240] The D-day to D+13 performance of the Bark beaches is detailed at Appendix G. In fact if anything, the logisticians had overestimated the maintenance needs of XXX Corps, delivering too much materiel too quickly to the beaches over that period. After-action reports are littered with instances of supply excesses in

97

particular of water, POL, ammunition, ordnance and Royal Engineers equipment.[241] However, in the complex business of calculating the needs of vast armies, risk adjusted for all manner of unforeseen eventualities, this is the side of the supply equation that campaign administrators always wish to be on.[242] In the case of Operation Husky, this achievement was made possible by enlightened forward planning, but also an ability to be agile in thought and flexible in local decision making, rather than sticking rigidly to a predetermined plan. The War Office report from August 1943 in its final summing up notes that:

> Finally, in a combined operation, even more than in any other phase of war, the best laid plans will go wrong. One sound and quick decision made on the beaches is worth one hundred pages of detailed plans made to cover every eventuality.[243]

Lord Louis Mountbatten, the Chief of Combined Operations, commented soon after the campaign that:

> Few lessons were learnt from the almost unopposed assault; the period of maintenance over the beaches however, we gained much experience. For the first time a large force was maintained for a period of 14 days over the beaches, using for lighterage the most modern craft and ambitions.[244]

Maintaining the Canadians in the Field

The 1 Canadian Infantry Brigade had been given Ispica as its Day+5 objective, a town approximately fourteen miles to the northwest of the Bark West beaches. They were far more successful than had been expected, however, and were at Ragusa on D+3, more than thirty-seven miles from their beach supply depots. Lt.-Col. W. P. Gilbride was the Assistant Adjutant and Quartermaster General (AA & QMG) of the 1 Canadian Infantry Brigade. He gave a lengthy post-action account of the maintenance of his brigade to Captain Sesia, the

Canadian historical officer, and the complete report has been sourced from the Canadian military archives.[245] Gilbride reports that the brigade faced two significant problems because of the pace of their advance both of which were inextricably connected: firstly, because so few stores were unloaded onto Beach 57 on D-day as discussed already, there was a concern they would run out of rations and POL by D+5; and secondly, the loss of the ninety-nine three ton trucks from the torpedoed ships had depleted First Line Transport resourcing and gave concern that, unless the pursuit of the enemy could be maintained, Axis forces might get an opportunity to dig in which could seriously jeopardise the whole campaign. Although XXX Corps would ultimately enjoy an embarrassment of supply largesse by D+14, the first ten days of the campaign would see supply shortfalls emerge which logisticians would need to fill.

1 Canadian Infantry Brigade had one day's combat rations on their vehicles as well as the emergency forty-eight hour rations they had been issued with but, in order to retain these reserve rations, they were going to need to draw rations from supply depots on D+1 to be consumed on D+2, and so on, which was far from ideal. This was the only option open to them, however, and the problem of transporting the rations fell to the Royal Canadian Army Service Corps (RCASC) which established a round-the-clock shuttle service between the Bark beach depots, where vehicles were loaded directly from off-loading landing craft, and the battle front.[246] The official British historian estimated that the ETF formations had only thirty per cent of their planned transport available to them between D-day and D+14 which might have presented a serious crisis.[247] The problem of transportation was addressed by the logisticians in three ways: firstly, RCASC used First Line Transport for their continuous relays in the first two days which meant that front line troops had to relinquish non-essential vehicles for POL and ration transportation; secondly, the brigade began to capture considerable numbers of enemy vehicles and the Royal Electrical and Mechanical Engineers (REME) set up repair workshops along the LofC by to get

these vehicles quickly serviced and redeployed; and thirdly, as the Canadians drove northwards towards Caltagirone on D+7 and encountered mountainous terrain which was unsuitable for mechanised transport, 1st Canadian Infantry Division Mule Transport Company was formed with trained Canadian muleteers overseeing 202 mules, forty horses and one donkey which had all been pressganged into Allied transport duty.[248]

As the advance of the front line slowed, the logisticians were able to establish a formal supply axis for the Canadians and a more reliable provision of materiel could be assured. A Forward Maintenance Centre (FMC)[249] was opened at Palazzolo on D+5 and subsequently at Scordia on D+14 but the distance by round trip at its longest, from the supply depots to the front line, was 225 miles. The RCASC, working in very close cooperation with the REME, manged to ensure that vehicles were on the road for twenty to twenty-two hours per day which was in any case just one round trip given the appalling driving conditions.[250] Despite all the challenges that were faced, the resourcefulness of the logisticians ensured that there was no break in the supply of essential materiel during that critical period. The advance of the ETF up to D+10, the 1st Canadian Infantry Division's supply axis and the position of the FMCs can be seen in Figure 14.

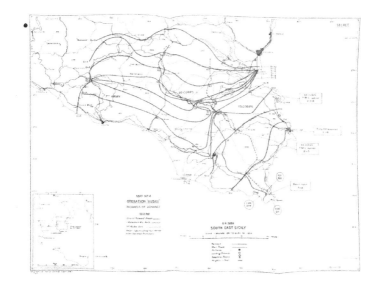

Figure 14
Progress of Advance of ETF up to D+10 [251]

Maintenance of the ETF in the Sicilian Campaign

The preceding section examined the maintenance of one division in Operation Husky during the first ten days of the campaign. This section will analyse the maintenance of the ETF as an army over the entire campaign and whether the efforts of the logisticians helped or hindered the capture of Sicily. It must be recognised that quite soon after 10 July, Eisenhower recognised that it was a matter of when and not if the island of Sicily would be reduced. He began training his eyes and those of his planners on the next Allied actions which were to be three separate invasions of mainland Italy in early September.[252] This presented a fresh challenge for the logisticians who had to plan now for three large and dispersed military exercises while at the same time continuing to ensure the integrity of the Husky LofCs. Decisions needed to be quickly made in particular as to where the centre of gravity of the LofC and supply depots to support these actions should be based: North Africa, Sicily or a combination of both.

Although the securing of the ETF's beach supply bridgeheads differed from sector to sector, the 1st Canadian Infantry Division's challenges being the greatest, all beach supply depots had been established on D-day. Sights were now set on securing key transportation infrastructure - ports, railways and airfields – in order to develop and underpin orthodox maintenance. As already mentioned, 1 Canadian Infantry Brigade secured the Pachino airfield by 0900hrs on D-day and, although it had been ploughed up by retreating Italian forces, an emergency landing strip had been completed by airfield construction engineers for the middle of the afternoon.[253] On D+5 the railway at Pachino was brought into operation and supplies began to be transported along the divisional supply axes to and from Syracuse with Scordia, sixty-seven miles to the northeast, opening on D+12.[254] The capture of the port of Syracuse was critical, however, for providing the bulk of the maintenance ambitions of the ETF as well as for delivering on the 1,000 tons per day supply commitment they had made to the United States WTF from D+14.[255] The city was occupied by 17 Infantry Brigade late on D-day and the following morning at 1000hrs the reconnaissance party of 86 LofC Area landed on the virtually intact quayside. It then established itself in the technical school in Syracuse and commenced the process of reopening the port in order to receive Allied ships and thereby anchor the ETF LofC.[256] The capture of this port, which would discharge a daily average of 3,830 tons of supplies for the remainder of the campaign, meant that the D+3 ETF convoys could now more safely discharge in port rather than over beaches as originally intended, a real coup for the logisticians.[257] The port of Augusta was also captured later on D+3 and maintained by HQ 151 Sub-Area although it wasn't until D+26 that Catania, the third port in southeastern Sicily, fell into Allied hands.

Operational logistics for the ETF became somewhat humdrum as the campaign progressed and supply lines were never put under the types of pressure they had experienced in the first fourteen days of the campaign, particularly as the Axis forces had decided on a staged withdrawal from the island from D+17. The ever decreasing and, therefore, more easily defended battle front meant that Allied supply lines lengthened ever more slowly towards Messina in the northeast and the final three weeks of the campaign were characterised by a well primed LofC transporting an abundance of materiel to its consumers, apart from a small number of exceptions.[258] The weekly administrative review at Appendix H demonstrates just how in control the ETF was of their supply situation. Fresh administrative orders were issued throughout the campaign at corps level which mandated particular operations, specified how maintenance would be organised and ensured that battle plans were aligned with logistical imperatives. For example, XXX Corps Administrative Order No. 89 was issued on 30 July to launch Operation Hardgate, a successful effort to break the Hauptkampflinie, the Axis line-of-resistance.[259] This order detailed the formations which would be involved in the action, how they and their supplies would be transported to the front and comprehensive manifests of rations, ammunition, ordnance, vehicles and POL.

As discussed in the previous chapter, phase three of the campaign from an administrative perspective was where the responsibility for maintenance of the ETF would move from HQ 86 Area, under the command of HQ XXX Corps, to HQ Fifteenth Army Group. This took place on D+6 far sooner than had been anticipated. As the so-called spearhead of the ETF, HQ 86 Area immediately moved north towards the battle front in order to reconnoitre the area around Catania from a maintenance perspective in anticipation of its capture.[260] Meanwhile on D+7, HQ Fortbase came into being in Syracuse, charged with the overall responsibility for the maintenance of Sicily, and reporting into HQ Fifteenth Army Group.[261] The final phase of the administrative plan quickly followed phase three, with the merging of the ETF and WTF's separate bases and axes of supply into consolidated bases, and so the centre of gravity of administrative control shifted to Sicily. On D+17, HQ Fortbase Administrative Instruction No. 1 was issued which defined the administrative control of the entire island for both armies. Although the campaign was only seventeen days old, the Allies had already established a solid LofC foundation with a growing number of FMCs and controlled ports, airfields and railways which could disembark plentiful supplies as can been in Figure 15.

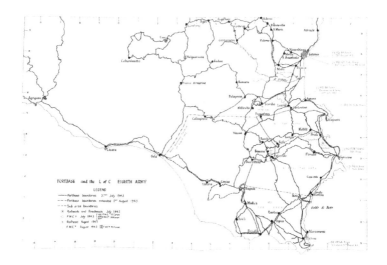

Figure 15
Fortbase and the LofC Eighth Army on D+17 [262]

Brigadier G. Surtees, the DA&QMG of GHQ MEF, visited the ETF between D+8 and D+13 and, on his return to Cairo, wrote a lengthy report on the general maintenance of the ETF:

> Until stiff German opposition was encountered south of Catania the whole operation progressed with astonishing success, and the administrative plans previously worked out were implemented with no major difficulties.[263]

He cited the 'efficiency and experience of the administrative services' as key to the outstanding success of the first fortnight of the campaign.

The final administrative order of the Sicilian campaign was issued by HQ Fortbase on 12 August with the majority of the instruction focused on the build-up of depots in Catania and Messina, which was still to be captured, for Operation Baytown.[264] The activities and focus of the logisticians, whose job in war is never truly done, had already moved on to the next phase of the Mediterranean campaign, the Allied invasion of mainland Italy.

Conclusions

The sinking of three convoy ships on the night of 4 and 5 July, and the consequent loss of vehicles, equipment and supplies, particularly rations, created an unanticipated challenge for XXX Corps. This threatened the success of the ETF's invasion plans and came close to eroding the margins of safety that the logisticians had incorporated into their maintenance calculations. When combined with the unhelpful physical features of Beach 57 and the inclement weather conditions, the fortunes of, in particular, the 1st Canadian Infantry Division were close to being fatally affected. In hindsight, Beach 57 should never have been designated as an assault beach and could be viewed as a failure of pre-invasion reconnaissance. The prize of the Pachino airfield was deemed too important to ignore, however, and Beach 57 was the closest one to that target. The potentially damaging logistical consequences were offset by experienced administrative heads who took local decisions based on arising intelligence rather than sticking rigidly to operational plans. The decision to move No. 4 Beach Group to Beach 56, reroute disembarking supplies, and sidestep beach groups northwards up the Sicilian coast proved to be an enlightened one. It demonstrated a flexibility of thought and action which typified the behaviour of the logisticians throughout this period. By the end of the campaign, Beach 56 was the most effective one used by the ETF and it was generally concluded that 'still larger tonnages could have been put into Sicily' from it and adjoining beaches if that had been required.[265]

While ultimately a boon to the fortunes of the Allied campaign in Sicily, the virtually unopposed landings by the ETF on the assault beaches created problems for the logisticians. They had to grapple with the challenges of priming a supply line which rapidly lengthened well beyond original estimates and was additionally hamstrung by a severely reduced transportation fleet. The resourcefulness and inventiveness of the logisticians was again evident by the speed with which they deployed a relay system using captured vehicles, pack transport and their own First Line Transport. It was a close-run thing at times in those critical first few days of the campaign but, with the close collaboration of Beach Groups, RSASC and REME, even the most challenged formation, 1 Canadian Infantry Brigade enjoyed uninterrupted deliveries of supplies. Apart from this particular situation, Allied formations were extremely well served by their logistics brethren throughout the campaign with a stable LofC delivering the necessary materiel of war. A conservative logistical ethos, where calculations were prudently risk adjusted with embedded margins of safety, had ensured that the ETF was able to achieve its objectives despite significant unplanned for complications and challenges.

Eisenhower, Alexander and the Allied naval and air chiefs, Air Marshall Tedder and Admiral Cunningham, came in for a lot of criticism in the post-campaign analysis, and from subsequent scholarly commentators, for allowing an Axis force of approximately 140,000 to escape to mainland Italy virtually unimpeded with all their equipment and vehicles. The Allied high command was preoccupied with the planning for the landings on mainland Italy at the time and missed their opportunity to cut off the Axis retreat by naval blockade and aerial bombardment. The escaping German formations were to subsequently form a core of resistance against the Allies when they embarked on their Italian mainland campaign. However, this missed opportunity was an operational and tactical one rather than a logistical one. A well-established LofC was in place early in the Operation Husky campaign and was in a position to support other actions if they had been mandated. By D+17, the full workings of the Allied logistics machine was established on the island and had swung into maintenance action. Administrative orders continued to be issued right up to the end of the campaign and remained critical to manage the scale of complexity of, not only the closing stages of the Operation Husky ground campaign, but also the preparations for the three Italian mainland invasions. Numerous after-action reports were commissioned at the end of the campaign so that lessons could be learned and applied to future amphibious exercises, as well as to later ground and air assaults. These reports recommended a plethora of operational tweaks and refinements to existing doctrine and highlighted that the Allied logisticians had increasingly become a learning organisation, willing and able to learn from their mistakes, adapt their working practices and thus improve.[266]

On 20 August, just three days after the Sicilian campaign had ended, Eisenhower sent a note to Gale (see Figure 16) where he speculates that in the future, the military critics will be:

> earnestly attempting to apportion credit for Allied victories in North Africa and Sicily. No matter what may be the nature of their conclusions, it is certain that all of us here keenly realise how definitely every one of our successes has been founded in the toil and sweat and brains of the Allied supply services.

ALLIED FORCE HEADQUARTERS
Office of the Commander-in-Chief

20 August, 1943.

TO: Lt. General Gale
Major General Hughes.

Dear General:

It is likely that for years to come the military critics will be earnestly attempting to apportion properly among the various arms the credit for Allied victories, to date, in North Africa and Sicily. No matter what may be the nature of their conclusions, it is certain that all of us here keenly realize how definitely every one of our successes has been founded in the toil and sweat and brains of the Allied Supply Services.

The three Commanders-in-Chief join with me in expressing to you and to all serving under you, our lasting appreciation as well as our sincere congratulations on your demonstrated efficiency.

Cordially,

Dwight D. Eisenhower

Lt. General H. M. Gale,
Chief Administrative Officer,
Allied Force Headquarters.

Figure 16

Note to Lt. General H. M. Gale, CAO AFHQ, from General Eisenhower, C-in-C Allied Forces, 20 August 1943 [267]

Chapter Five
A Triumph over Immense Odds

The Allied invasion of Sicily on 10 July 1943 was the largest and most dispersed amphibious assault of the Second World War. It was also the most complex combined operations logistics exercise attempted by the Allies up to that point in the war with an initial assault force comprising 176,000 soldiers, landing across a one hundred mile span of southeastern Italy. The best way to contextualise the logistical degree of difficulty associated with Operation Husky is to compare it with Operation Overlord, the invasion of France in June 1944. The Normandy landings comprised an invasion force of 156,000 soldiers on D-day, landing across a fifty mile assault front. Normandy planners had fifteen months to prepare for battle, with a stable, experienced and properly empowered planning team in place, were able to assemble their invasion force from a home base and then faced a short sea crossing to France from a well defended shore. In addition, the Allied commanders and their troops were available well in advance to prepare both operationally and tactically for the invasion of France. Operation Husky, on the other hand, was just five months in the making, with an inexperienced planning team and a dysfunctional organisational structure, was assembled from multiple locations across the Mediterranean, the United States and Britain, and the armada had to traverse two hundred and fifty miles of hostile, open water to reach the invasion destination. To complicate matters further, Husky commanders and the majority of their divisions were engaged in the Tunisian war until less than two months before the invasion date, leaving them precious little time for rest, training or tactical preparation. Even so, in late July 1943, an armada comprising 2,590 vessels set sail from multiple locations across the Mediterranean as well as directly from Britain and the United States. Significant logistical challenges had been overcome so that 176,000 soldiers could be landed on the beaches of southeastern Sicily on 10 July 1943 with 14,000 vehicles, 600 tanks and 1,800 guns. A combined operations beach landing and beach maintenance exercise of this magnitude had never been attempted before and yet over the course of fourteen days, a total of 467,000 soldiers would be deployed on the island, equipped with the necessary equipment and stores to prosecute the campaign. From D+1 to D+14, 88,872 tons of supplies were discharged over the beaches and a further 12,556 vehicles were shipped to the island. All the after-action reports for Operation Husky agree that maintenance could have been continued over the beaches indefinitely if the ports of Syracuse and Palermo had not been captured. And, apart from some very minor and fleeting supply line gaps, the Allies enjoyed an abundance of materiel throughout the period up to the capture of the island.

This book set out to assess the role that the logistics of the British ETF played in the Operation Husky campaign from the Casablanca conference in January 1943, through the planning, embarkation and invasion phases until the reduction of the island of Sicily in August 1943. A review of the existing literature, discussed in the introduction to this thesis, shows that although much has been written about the campaign itself, there is a dearth of scholarly study on the logistical aspects of the campaign. There is virtually no analysis on the role, if any, that combined operations logistics might have played in the success of the campaign. To add insult to injury, the British and Canadian historians charged with the faithful recording of their countries' exploits in Sicily, both state in their respective introductions that, while they recognised the part played by the supporting services in the campaign, they would be unable to devote any effort to investigating them further. They cited the enormity of the exercise that it would require and said that their account, therefore, must necessarily be restricted. Campaign success is attributed to both the overwhelming Allied force and the lack of Sicilian and German resistance, although more detailed analysis tends to focus on criticising the Allies for their poor planning, their lack of cohesion and the missed opportunity to capture retreating Axis forces. Such an approach to the reporting of war by the official historians is unsatisfactory. Of equal concern is the inability of successive historians and scholarly commentators to challenge the assertions of the official narrative. By failing to explore the role of logistics in the campaign, there is a genuine concern that our understanding of the key drivers and influences behind the success of Operation Husky is incomplete. Winston Churchill, writing in *The River War* in 1899, appealed to military students to be ever mindful of not ignoring the less glamorous, but no less crucial, aspect of military study that is logistics:

> In a tale of war the reader's mind is filled with the fighting. The battle - with its vivid scenes, its moving incidents, its plain and tremendous results - excites imagination and commands attention...The long trailing line of communications is unnoticed. The fierce glory that plays on red, triumphant bayonets dazzles the observer; nor does he care to look behind to where, along a thousand miles of rail, road, and river, the convoys are crawling to the front in unnoticed succession. Victory is the beautiful bright-coloured flower. Transport is the stem without which it could never have blossomed. Yet even the military student, in his zeal to master the fascinating combinations of the actual conflict, often forgets the far more intricate complications of supply.[268]

Unfortunately, it appears that Husky scholars were either unaware of, or have ignored, this important advice and, as a result of a serious oversight, the role of logistics in the Sicily campaign has been completely obscured and comprehensively misunderstood. The assertion is made, in fact, that the logistics of the campaign were not just one of the factors behind the success of Operation Husky, but the principal one. The case for this assertion has been built through the preceding chapters.

Chapter two asked what logistical challenges were created for the British ETF by the tortuous planning process. Operation Husky was a monumental exercise for the logisticians, even without the complicating factors which were to emerge during the preparations for the invasion. The first of these was the fact that the preliminary plan conceived by the British JPS was both operationally flawed and technically unsound and went through seven significant iterations in just four months before the final version was agreed. Even then, there were no post-Husky objectives included in the agreed plan and it was decided that any further military activity would be at the sole discretion of General Eisenhower to decide as the invasion of Sicily evolved. A miscalculation in the JPS plan with respect to the shipping needs of Husky, coupled with a global shortage in the availability of specialised invasion craft, threatened the invasion as late as April 1943. In order to free up the necessary capacity, Britain had to run down the reserves of the home fleet to the bare minimum compatible with safety and this additionally put paid to the chances of an amphibious Normandy operation later in 1943, which the Allies had been preparing for.

The Husky planning structure proved to be structurally defective. It lacked a senior individual at its head and the senior support to make decisions, and it soon came into conflict with the already established AFHQ and GHQ MEF organisations. To complicate matters further, the distraction of the Tunisian war, which dragged through April and into May, meant that the individuals who should have been preparing for the next war, were still fighting the last one. As a result, decisions on important matters drifted for days and weeks before operational commanders could meet with planners and logisticians to make progress. The very late substitution of UK-based Canadian forces in place of the British 3rd Division in the Husky battle order, while politically expedient, caused additional headaches for the logisticians in London and in the Mediterranean. The most significant challenge, however, was a yawning leadership void which emerged within the Allied ranks between the Allied high command, the three services, and the planners. Alexander and Eisenhower must bear significant responsibility for the confusion which reigned during this period. They failed to manage their respective work-loads effectively and the cumulative impact of the complications created a monumental task for those charged with the responsibility of administering and maintaining the campaign. It is not unreasonable to suppose that, without the responsible intervention of experienced individuals, Operation Husky could have resulted in a disastrous outcome.

Into this leadership void stepped the Husky logisticians and the third chapter examined how they met the planning challenges up to the ETF landings on 10 July. Although inter-Allied and inter-service cooperation was in its infancy in early 1943, the British logistics doctrine and its organisational capability were at an advanced stage of development. This experience had been hard won in the North African campaign and the logisticians had not only become closely bonded with the front-line commanders as essential participants in the planning and execution of war, they had also become familiar with the various idiosyncrasies and proclivities of their colleagues. Thus, the type of planning challenges and uncertainties that Operation Husky threw up, although on a scale they hadn't previously had to cope with, were not totally unfamiliar to them. Rather than waiting for perfectly formed plans to emerge from the top and trickle down to them, the logisticians went ahead with the business of preparing for war and managed their business from the bottom up. Although the invasion plan was not finalised until 3 May, the logisticians brought much-needed stability and direction to the campaign preparations in the midst of the planning mayhem. Logistical coherence was provided through the issuance of a series of Maintenance and Administration Plans from 9 March onwards. These were immensely detailed and comprehensive documents which gave military formations everything they needed to prepare for the invasion. The primary archives contain substantial amounts of information on Operation Husky and its administrative preparations. Hundreds of files provide meticulous recordings of, for instance, loading schedules, ships' manifests, and projected maintenance statistics which this study shows a brief glimpse of in the appendices. Every successful human enterprise, be it military or commercial, which operates on a grand scale with inherent organisational complexity, is successful because accurate data is at the heart of that organisation and is available to its leaders, who in turn have a fluency with this data. The ETF resembled a sophisticated procurement and supply-chain organisation, with a solid foundation anchored in accurate, relevant and concise data, operating under the direction of experienced data analysts.. The precision, accuracy and completeness of the detail that was contained in the various administrative orders that were issued, gave the quartermaster network that ran through the spine of the ETF, everything they needed to ready their formations for the invasion. Possibly the most complex embarkation task faced by the ETF logisticians was the transportation and embarkation of XXX Corps, its troops, stores and vehicles, from across the Mediterranean and the Middle East. This exercise proceeded with metronomic efficiency and, during June, 65,693 troops, 9,442 vehicles and 60,111 tons of stores were moved to the ports of Benghazi, Suez, Haifa, Beirut and Alexandria by road, rail and sea. It is difficult to imagine Operation Husky could have even been staged without the contribution of the logisticians.

New organisational approaches for combined operations were evolved by the logisticians in advance of Operation Husky to address the over-the-beach maintenance challenges which had emerged during Operation Torch. A formation called a Beach Group was established, consisting of up to 3,000 men of all ranks, with up to twenty different units and services working together. Engineer, medical, artillery and signal detachments as well as naval Beach Masters and army landing officers were established within individual infantry battalions. The assaulting division would have the responsibility of the Beach Group during the assault phase and help in establishing the beachhead supply depots, as well as the fledgling LofC, before passing this responsibility to the Army Group HQ when it arrived on the island. Another innovation, and a measure of how the logisticians were prepared to embrace technological advances, was the deployment of the DUKW at Operation Husky. Without these amphibious vehicles, it is debatable whether the ETF could have ultimately been supplied over beaches as successfully as it was. After-action reports deemed Beach Bricks and DUKWs to be particular successes and they subsequently became essential components of the maintenance plans for the Normandy landings in June 1944. In summary, if the logistics capability of the ETF had been as dysfunctional as the planning capability of the Allies, the invasion of Sicily might have been calamitous.

The fourth chapter analysed how the logistics of the British ETF helped the capture of Sicily from the invasion date onwards. Helmuth von Moltke the Elder, Chief of Staff of the Prussian General Staff in 1857, said that 'no plan of operations extends with any certainty beyond the first contact with the main hostile force' and this was to be the case for Operation Husky.[269] In fact, two significant challenges emerged for the ETF prior to the invasion date which tested the resourcefulness of the logisticians and the quality of the safety margins embedded in their calculations. The first challenge was when KMS19, the slow convoy transporting part of the 1st Canadian Infantry Division from the UK, was attacked on the night of 4 and 5 July by U-boats off the North African coast. Three ships were torpedoed and the ETF lost most of its Second Line of Transport vehicles, rations for D+2 and beyond, as well as significant amounts of signal equipment. The second challenge was the offshore topography of Beach 57 at Pachino peninsula which had been assigned to land part of the Canadian division. It had numerous false beaches and about fifty-five per cent of the LCMs carrying troops on D-day, as well as forty per cent of the LCMs carrying supplies on D+1, were stranded on these sandbars. While the assault troops were ultimately landed on Beach 57, albeit one hour and forty-four minutes late, these two developments created an early maintenance crisis for the logisticians. They faced a shortage of vital supplies and Second Line Transport, and an assault beach which appeared that it would significantly underperform plans for its discharge abilities. However, the logisticians showed admirable coolness under battle-field pressure and an ability to solve the problems thrown their way. Rather than sticking rigidly to operational plans, a local decision was taken based on arising intelligence. It was decided to decommission Beach 57 and sidestep the beach group capability up the coast to Beach 56 which was already outperforming its pre-invasion discharge estimates. This proved to be an enlightened decision as Beach 56 was the most effective one used by the ETF for disembarking supplies in Sicily and it was generally concluded that still larger tonnages could have been landed if that had been required. This demonstrated not only flexibility of thought and action on the part of the logisticians at critical points in the campaign, but also the inherent robustness of their plans which incorporated contingency measures should circumstances require them.

Although the beach maintenance crisis was ultimately averted by the logisticians, they were faced with a much more immediate LoC challenge. Owing to the paucity of Axis resistance in southeastern Sicily, 1 Canadian Infantry Brigade stretched its supply line to a length of thirty-seven miles by D+3, more than three times as long as had been anticipated. The brigade faced two significant maintenance problems due to the pace of their advance; firstly, because so few stores had been unloaded onto Beach 57 on D-day, there was a pressing concern that they would run out of combat rations and POL by D+5; and secondly, formations had only thirty per cent of their Second Line Transport available to them owing to the KMS19 torpedo attack. Displaying admirable resourcefulness, a round-the-clock shuttle service was established by the logisticians between the Bark beach depots and the battle front using non-essential First Line Transport as well as captured and repaired enemy vehicles. As the brigade began to encounter mountainous terrain, 1st Canadian Infantry Division Mule Transport Company was deployed to supplement mechanised transportation and ensure the continuity of the supply line. These actions ensured that there was no break in the supply of essential materiel. If invasion momentum had stalled at this critical juncture, it would have jeopardised the capture of the island.

Despite these challenges, all beach supply depots for the ETF had been established on D-day and over-the-beach maintenance continued at pace. Sights were quickly set on securing key transportation infrastructure, ports and airfields, in order to develop and underpin orthodox maintenance. Administrative orders continued to be issued right up to the end of the campaign and remained critical to manage the scale of complexity of, not only the closing stages of Operation Husky ground campaign, but also the preparations for the three mainland Italy invasions, scheduled for early September. On D+17, HQ Fortbase Administrative Instruction No. 1 was issued which defined the administrative control of the entire island for both armies. Although the campaign was only seventeen days old, the logisticians had already established a solid LofC foundation with a growing number of FMCs. They controlled ports, airfields and railways, and could disembark plentiful supplies onto the island, providing front line commanders with unlimited operational flexibility to support whatever action that was necessary to capture the island.

The purpose of this academic work was to determine the role that the logistics of the British Eastern Task Force played in the invasion of Sicily. It finds that Operation Husky was a triumph of British combined operations logistics over immense odds. In fact, the logisticians deserve the principal credit, among all the actors involved, for the role they played in the success of the campaign. They displayed considerable maturity, leadership and foresight in coping with the complications created by a chaotic planning period. Their approach throughout was prudent and framed within conservative operational safety margins. At the same time, they embraced innovation and were able to show agility and resourcefulness when faced with unforeseen challenges. This study therefore asserts that the role of logistics in the preparation and execution of the campaign was a monumental achievement and was the defining factor in the capture of Sicily in August 1943. Such an assertion potentially necessitates a substantial revision of the accepted understanding of the role and importance of logistics in the success of, not only Operation Husky, but of all subsequent amphibious operations in the Second World War. Notwithstanding the achievements of the Allies in Sicily, no scholarly connection appears to have been made between the combined operations achievements of Husky and the successful invasion of France in June 1944. If the findings of this study are to be accepted, the logistical achievements of Operation Husky were in fact a defining event in the Second World War. Viewed through this prism, the D-day landings at Normandy were essentially trialled at Sicily when vital logistical and organisational foundations were established for the invasion of France just ten months later. Operation Husky was a defining event in the Second World War and it is hoped that this book will lead to a better understanding of the role that British logistics played in winning the war in Europe.

Appendices

Appendix A.
Combined Chiefs of Staff Memo
System of Command for Combined U.S.-British Operations [270]

U. S. SECRET
BRITISH MOST SECRET
C.C.S. 75/3

October 24, 1942

COMBINED CHIEFS OF STAFF

SYSTEM OF COMMAND FOR COMBINED U. S.-BRITISH OPERATIONS
(Previous reference: (a) C.C.S. 38th Meeting, Item 3)

Report by Combined Staff Planners

1.   The enclosure, prepared by the Combined Staff Planners in accord-ance with reference (a), is presented for consideration by the Combined Chiefs of Staff. Annex "A", attached thereto, presents graphically the principles of unified command as contained in the report.

2.   The U. S. Navy members of the Combined Staff Planners state that while this paper does not in its entirety accord with their views, it is believed that it presents the best agreement which can be reached at this time. The U. S. Navy members believe that the status of the assistants to Supreme Commander, because of the possible interpretation of their func-tions, may result in actually interposing an additional element in the chain of command which would limit the authority of the Supreme Commander.

ENCLOSURE

SYSTEM OF UNIFIED COMMAND FOR COMBINED OPERATIONS

DEFINITIONS:

1.   Unified command is the control, exercised by a designated com-mander, over a force integrated from combined and joint forces allocated to him for the accomplishment of a mission or task. This force will include all the means considered necessary for the mission's successful execution. Unified command vests in the designated commander, the re-sponsibility and authority to control the operations of all arms and services composing his force, by the organization of task forces, as-signment of missions, designation of objectives, and the exercise of such control as he deems necessary to insure the success of his mission. Unified command does not authorize the commander exercising it, to control the administration and discipline of any forces of the United

1

119

Nations composing his command, beyond those necessary for effective
control.

2.   The term "joint" refers to participation of forces from two or
more of the *arms* (U. S.) or *services* (British) of one nation.

3.   The term "combined" refers to the participation of *forces* of two
or more of the United Nations.

SUPREME COMMANDER:

4.   In cases where the governments concerned so decide, a Supreme
Commander will be appointed for operations when forces of more than one
of the United Nations are to be employed on a specific mission or task.

5.   He will be appointed by agreement between the governments concerned at the earliest possible moment after the decision to undertake
an operation has been made.

6.   He will exercise unified command over all forces of the United
Nations allocated to his operation.

7.   He will be the recipient of all major directives pertaining to
the arms and services of his force.

8.   Out of the means allocated to him, he will organize task forces
as necessary, designate their commanders, and assign the major tasks to
be performed by each.

9.   He will be assisted by a small composite staff which will include
in principle a Chief of Staff, a Planning Division, an Operations Division, an Intelligence Division, a Logistical Division, and a Communications Center. Each nation involved and each of the several component
arms or services of the force will be represented on the staff in order
to insure an understanding of the capabilities, requirements, and limitations of each component.

LAND, NAVAL AND AIR COMMANDERS:

10.   The officer appointed by the Combined Chiefs of Staff as the
Senior Officer of each combined arm or service not specifically allocated
to task forces by the Supreme Commander, will advise the Supreme Commander on the best use of his own combined arm or service.

11.   These Commanders will carry out their duties at the headquarters
of the Supreme Commander unless specifically ordered otherwise by him.

TASK FORCE COMMANDERS:

12.   Task Force Commanders will organize their commands as may be
necessary for the execution of the tasks assigned. Sub-Task Force

2

Commanders will be designated as may be necessary for the execution of the subordinate tasks assigned. The principle of unified command will apply throughout.

13.   The organization of task forces will be governed by the nature of the operations to be performed. The task forces will include all the elements--land, air and naval--necessary for the accomplishment of the task. The appointment of the Task Force Commanders, subordinate as well as major, will be governed by the nature of the task assigned, and the major arm or service involved in its performance, i.e., whether preponderantly land, air or naval.

INTEGRITY OF NATIONAL UNITS:

14.   Insofar as conditions will permit, task forces will be composed of units of the same nationality. When organizations of one nation serve under the command of an officer of another, the principle will be maintained that such organizations shall be kept intact and not scattered among other units.

3

121

ANNEX "A"

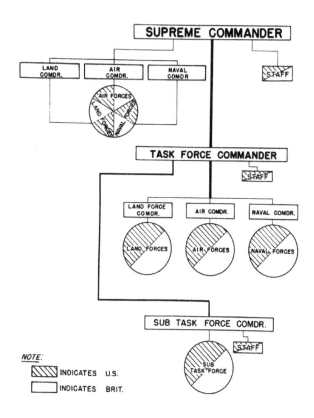

Appendix B.
Administrative Planning Instruction No. 1
Provisional Allotment of Shipping to Destinations [271]

PROVISIONAL ALLOTMENT OF SHIPPING TO DESTINATIONS.

PART I.

ACID NORTH (H.Q. SHIP - BULOLO)

Ships	Personnel	Vehs	Tanks	LCP	LCA	LCM	LCS
D DAY							
1 LSI(M) - Ulster Monarch	400	-	-	-	5	-	1
5 LSI(L) - Duchess of Bedford (SNOL)	3160	-	-	-	11	-	1
Sobieski	1684	-	-	-	10	1	1
Monarch of Bermuda	2594	-	-	-	12	-	-
Reina del Pacifico (SNOL)	2520	-	-	-	14	1	1
Tegelburg	2179	-	-	-	10	-	-
3 LSP - Dilwara	1600	-	-	10	-	-	-
Dunera	1600	-	-	10	-	-	-
Bergensfiord	2113	-	-	-	-	-	-
1 LSC - Empire Charmian	50	30	-	-	-	21	-
15 MT/Stores Ships	3450	1800	-	-	-	36	-
8 LST	1200	72	98	-	-	-	-
24 LCT	720	240	-	-	-	-	-
TOTAL LIFT =	23250	2142	98	20	62	59	4

PLUS 12 LCI(L) arrive empty.

Ships	Personnel	Vehs	Tanks	LCP	LCA	LCM	LCS
D plus 3 DAY							
LSP to give a lift of	11000	-	-	-	-	-	-
6 LSP - Orbita	2221						
Aorangi	2576						
Leopoldville	1833						
Almanzora	1612						
Rohna	1520						
Rsgula	1600						
19 MT/Stores Ships	2850	2280					
TOTAL LIFT =	14212	2280	-	-	-	-	-

PART II.

ACID SOUTH

Ships	Personnel	Vehs	Tanks	LCP	LCA	LCM	LCS
D DAY							
1 LSI(S) - Prinz Albert	300	-	-	-	6	-	-
2 LSI(L) - Winchester Castle (SNOL)	1158	-	-	-	12	2	1
Orontes	3440	-	-	-	14	-	1
3 LSP - Devonshire	1440	-	-	10	-	-	-
Ruys	2226	-	-	10	-	-	-
Sibajak	1960	-	-	-	-	-	-
1 LSG - Ennerdale	50	21	-	-	-	15	-
9 MT/Stores Ships	2000	1080	-	-	-	20	-
6 LST	900	54	78	-	-	-	-
16 LCT	480	160	-	-	-	-	-
TOTAL LIFT =	13954	1315	78	20	32	37	2

PLUS 10 LCI(L) arriving empty.

Ships	Personnel	Vehs	Tanks	LCP	LCA	LCM	LCS
D plus 3 DAY							
4 LSP - CHR Hygene	2113						
to be nominated	1600						
" " "	1040						
" " "	1040						
10 MT/Stores Ships	1500	1200					
TOTAL LIFT =	7293	1200	-	-	-	-	-

(xii)

Appendix 'B'.

(contd.) PROVISIONAL ALLOTMENT OF SHIPPING TO DESTINATIONS.

BARK EAST (H.Q. SHIP - LARGE)

Ships	Personnel	Vehs	Tanks	LCP	LCA	LCM	LCS
D DAY	**PART I.**						
Keren BNOL	920	-	-	2	9	2	1
LSI (L) Otranto	3320	-	-	2	11	-	1
Strathnaver	3488	-	-	-	14	-	2
6 MT/Stores	1410	720	-	-	-	18	-
1 LST	150	3	15	-	-	-	-
8 LCT	240	80	-	-	-	-	-
	9528	803	15	4	34	20	4
	PLUS 4 LCI(L) arriving empty.						
D plus 3 DAY.							
1 MT/Store	150	120	-	-	-	-	-

PART II.

BARK WEST - - CDN DIV

(H.Q. SHIP - HILARY) FORCE 'X'.

Ships	Personnel	Vehs	Tanks	LCP	LCA	LCM	LCS
D DAY							
LSI(L)- Durban Castle	2022	-	-	-	14	-	-
Circassia BNOL	2016	-	-	-	16	-	-
Marnix	2809	-	-	-	14	-	-
Derbyshire	2566	-	-	-	16	-	2
Llangibby Castle	1736	-	-	-	18	-	-
Glengyle (SFOL)	982	-	-	-	11	3	1
	Total assault capacity for Army 687						
1 LSC Empire Elaine	50	31	-	-	-	21	-
1 LSG Derwentdale	50	21	-	-	-	14	-
12 LST	360	120	-	Based on FINANCE, probable load Amphibians and Drivers.			
8 LST	1200	24	96	-	-	-	-
14 MT/Stores	4200	1680	-	-	-	28	-
	17991	1876	96	-	89	66	3
	PLUS 3 LCT arriving with RAF vehicles from FINANCE and 8 LCI(L) arriving empty.						
D plus 3 DAY.							
LSP - Ascania 2291 / Batory 1663 / Empire Pride 1836	5790	-	-	10	-	-	-
14 MT/Stores	700	1680	-	-	-	-	-
2 additional LSP suggested with lift of 3800	3800	-	-	-	-	-	-
	10290	1680	-	10	-	-	-

(xiii)

Appendix 'B'.

PART II. (contd.)

(contd.) **BARK WEST** — **CDN DIV.**

FORCE 'Y'

TO BE HELD IN RESERVE IN N.A.

IMMEDIATE RESERVE.	Personnel.	Vehicles	Tanks.
LSP to lift	8250	-	-
6 LST	900	95	90
6 MT/Stores	300	720	-
	9450	815	90

FOLLOW UP FOR FUSTIAN.			
LSP to lift	5500	-	-
6 MT/Stores	300	720	-
GRAND TOTAL ...	15250	1535	90

PART III.

BARK SOUTH — **51 DIV.**
From AGOUTI, LAURAGH and HASHISH Staging at FINANCE.

Ships	Personnel	Vehs	Tanks	Stores	LCA	LCM	LCS
D DAY.							
LSI(M)							
Royal Scotsman)							
Royal Ulsterman)	1600	-	-	-	22	2	2
Queen Emma)							
Princess Beatrix)							
29 LST	4350	1163	69	-	-	-	-
18 LCT	540	180	-	-	-	-	-
10 LCT	300	-	-	1500	-	-	-
43 LCI(L)	8600	-	-	-	-	-	-
	15390	1343	69	1500	22	2	2
1st Follow up from FINANCE.							
21 LST	3150	1050	-	-	-	-	-
10 LCT	300	100	-	-	-	-	-
10 LCT	300	-	-	1500	-	-	-
30 LCI(L)	6000	-	-	-	-	-	-
	9750	1150	-	1500	-	-	-

Stores maintenance thereafter by 14 LCT from LAURAGH
and HASHISH on a four day turnround. Remaining
craft available for ferrying personnel and vehicles.

(xiv)

Appendix C.
Administrative Planning Instruction No. 1
Detail of Anti-malarial Precautions [272]

Appdx. 'R'.

SPECIAL COMMODITIES.

1. (a) Units will draw the following items of R.A.S.C. supply prior to embarkation, and will distribute to detachments in accordance with the Embarkation Table:-

ITEM	SCALE TO BE DRAWN BY UNIT	
AL 63	19 lbs.	
Cresol	½ gall.	
Sodium Arsenite	1½ ozs.	per
Fly catchers	10	100 men
Anti-mosquito cream	18½ lbs.	
Flysol	1½ galls.	

(b) Subsequent demands will be based on the M.E. scale (vide WE GO 21/43) with the following exceptions:-

ITEM	SCALE
(i) Sodium Arsenite	3 ozs. per 100 men per month.
(ii) Flysol	3 galls." " " " "
(iii) Barium Carbonate	Rat Exterminator will be drawn in lieu on the scale of 1½ ozs. per 100 men per month. Should Barium Carbonate be drawn the scale of issue will be 3/8ths oz. per 100 men per month.

(c) In addition the following special items will be drawn through R.A.S.C. channels prior to embarkation by all units:-

ITEM	SCALE
(i) Sterilising powder	6 lbs. per 1,000 men per month.
(ii) Water sterilising outfits	1 per N.C.O.
(iii) Mepacrine	8 tablets per man (14 days supply)
(iv) Taste Remover Tablets	260 boxes tablets per 1,000 men per month

NOTE: This will be issued with the sterilising powder.

(d) BEACH BRICKS will carry in addition to items in (a), (b) and (c) above:-

Creosote oil ... 8 galls. per BRICK.

2. The following are items of R.A.O.C. Supply to be carried by units:-

ITEM	SCALE
Fly swatters	10% of unit strength.
Flit guns	10% " "
Butter muslin } ...	As required, for flyproofing considered
Fish netting	essential before embarkation and certified by M.O.

(xv)

126

Appendix D.
Administrative Planning Instruction No. 1
Pre-embarkation Personnel and Stores Movements [273]

PERSONNEL AND STORES MOVED TO AND EMBARKED AT

MIDDLE EAST PORTS FOR "HUSKY".

- - S U M M A R Y - -

PERSONNEL.

	Offs.	ORs.	TOTAL	Sub-Appdx.
Embarked in Personnel Ships:-				
"D" Convoy	2,057	29,567	31,624	"D"
"D" Convoy (N.M. Ships)	138	1,559	1,797	"D"
"D" plus 3" Convoy	741	14,018	14,759	"D"
Embarked in L.S.Ts.	100	2,207	2,307	"E"
L.C.Ts.	110	2,583	2,693	"E"
Embarked in M.T. Stores Ships:-				
"D" Convoy	191	6,537	6,728	"F"
"D plus 3" Convoy	130	4,655	4,785	"F"
	3,467	61,126	65,693	

STORES AND VEHICLES LOADED.	Stores	Vehs.	M/Cs.	Sub-Appdx.
M.T. Stores Ships:-	Tons			
"D" Convoy	12,350	3,558	292	"B" & "F"
"D plus 3" Convoy	47,761	4,367	294	"B" & "F"
L.S.Ts.		651		"E"
L.C.Ts.		846		"E"
	60,111	9,422	586	

PRINCIPAL MOVES BY RAIL AND ROAD.	All Ranks	Vehs.	Sub-Appdx.
By Rail to TOBRUCH / Road to BENGHAZI	1,665	589	"A"
By Road to BENGHAZI	488	226	"A"
By Rail to SUEZ for embarkation (exercise)	7,609	-	"G"
By Rail to SUEZ for embarkation	43,094	-	"G"
By Rail to ALEXANDRIA (MALTA)	3,918	-	"C"
By Road to HAIFA	-	2,138	"H"
By Road to BEIRUT	-	1,857	"H"
By Road to ALEXANDRIA	-	3,930	"C"

(i)

Sub-Appendix "A".

<u>PERSONNEL AND VEHICLES RAIL TO TOBRUCH - ROAD TO BENGHAZI</u>

FOR EMBARKATION IN L.S.TS.

<u>BY RAIL</u>

<u>From 29th May to 13th June.</u>

Area FROM	TO	"A" Veh.	"B" Veh.	Misc.	Personnel
LEVANT	TOBRUCH	73	-	23	270
ALEXANDRIA	"	19	-	3	54
CAIRO	"	26	14	8	206
CANAL	"	103	132	188	1,135

TOTAL: 589 Vehicles
1,665 Personnel

<u>BY ROAD</u>

<u>From 8th to 13th June</u>

FAYID	BENGHAZI	-	137	89	488

TOTAL: 488 Personnel
226 Vehicles

(11)

SUB APPENDIX 'B'

D DAY CONVOY

STORES SHIPPING

Priority	SHIP	POL	AMN	R.E. STORES	ORD. STORES	RAF STORES	R.N. STORES	WATER	MISC. STORES	SUPPLIES	TOTALS	LOADING DATE	PORT X
		Tons	Tons	Tons	Tons	Tons	Tons	Tons	Tons	Tons	Tons		
A	TARANTIA	38¼	69	21½	1	13¼	6¼	-	16	-	165¾	5-8/6	B
A	OKARDA	40½	69	32¾	1½	¾	6	-	10	-	160¾	4-8/6	B
A	GEORGE R. CLARKE	41	66¾	3½	1	5 cwt.	4½	-	17	-	133¾	4-7/6	H
A	HARPAGUS	37¼	69	37	1	-	11	-	10	-	165¼	4-8/6	B
A	FRANK B. KELLOGG	42½	70	36	1	-	6	-	10	-	165½	5-8/6	B
A	JOSEPH G. CANNON	46	62	8¼	1½	-	3	-	16	-	137	5-7/6	H
A	LESLIE M. SHAW	43	118	11½	1½	-	4½	-	17	-	195¼	5-7/6	H
A	BIGFOOT WALLACE	43	64¼	5¾	1	-	4	-	10	-	128	4-7/6	H
B	O. HENRY	173	202¼	39½	2	-	-	77	10	86½	590½	9-13/6	H
B	COLIN P. KELLY	174	201½	45	3¼	-	-	76½	-	73	573¼	9-13/6	H
B	HIGHLAND PRINCE	234	248	57½	2	-	-	102	-	110	753½	2-8/6	B
B	GEORGE H. DEARN	175	199	49½	1½	-	-	77	10	138	650½	9-13/6	H
B	PIO PICO	232	260	58	1	-	-	103	10	110	774	9-15/6	B
B	MAYO BROS	174	155	53½	½	-	-	77	10	82	555	2-7/6	H
B	POCOHONTAS	243	261	58	1	-	-	103	10	110	706	9-15/6	B
A	OCEAN PRIDE	44¾	68¼	23	-	¼	5¼	-	9¼	-	151½	4-9/6	A
A	OCEAN STRENGTH	44¼	68½	23	¼	¼	5¼	-	9¼	-	152	4-9/6	A
A	OCEAN VULCAN	44½	71½	22¼	¼	¼	5½	-	9¼	-	155	4-9/6	A
A	OCEAN HUNTER	114¼	71¼	22¼	¼	¼	5¼	-	9¼	-	228¼	4-10/6	A
B	OCEAN PEACE	253	225½	60¼	2¼	-	-	76	4	63¼	685	10-16/6	A
B	OCEAN VALLEY	183¼	236	60¼	2¼	-	-	76	4	61½	623¾	9-15/6	A
B	BAARN	137	237¼	60¼	3¼	-	-	56	10	61	565¾	4-10/6	A
B	JONATHAN GROUT	261½	233½	60¼	3¼	-	-	76	4	60¼	699¾	10-15/6	A
B	BENJAMIN GOODHUE	204¼	233½	60¼	3¼	18¼	-	76	12	61	669¼	4-15/6	A
A	SHAHJEHAN	23½	72½	19	-	-	-	23	4	3	144¾	4-9/6	A
A	OCEAN GLORY	22½	70	27	-	19¼	-	19	12	3	172¾	4-9/6	A
B	THISTLEMUIR	148¼	216¼	29½	6¼	-	-	98	12	58	569	4-14/6	A
B	JOSEPH ALSTON	269	225½	22½	5½	-	-	112½	11	91½	696¾	9-15/6	A
B	FORT LAWRENCE	215¼	229¾	27½	5½	-	-	115	4	57	654	11-15/6	A
A	OCEAN VISION	129¼	75½	10	-	¼	-	29¾	4	2	251¾	4-9/6	A
	TOTAL ...	3833¾	4451	1047½	58¼	54¼	66¾	1372¾	275	1191¼	12349¾		

X PORTS:- A = ALEXANDRIA

B = BEIRUT

H = HAIFA

APPENDIX 'B'.

D PLUS 3 DAY CONVOY.

STORES SHIPMENT

Prio-ity	SHIP	POL	AMN	R.E. STORES	ORD STORES	RAF STORES	R.N. STORES	WATER	MISC. STORES	SUPPLIES	TOTALS	LOADING DATE	PORT X
		Tons	Tons	Tons	Tons	Tons	Tons	Tons	Tons	Tons	Tons		
A	GENA	89	40¼	-	-	-	-	-	10	-	139¼	10-12/6	B
A	DEBRETT	100	40½	-	-	-	-	-	10	-	150½	10-13/6	B
A	CHARLES G. CURTIS	98¼	40	-	-	-	-	-	10	-	148¼	21-22/6	H
A	ABRAHAM LINCOLN	100	40	-	-	-	-	-	10	-	150	10-11/6	H
A	RALPH IZARD	100	40	-	-	-	-	-	10	-	150	10-12/6	H
A	JOHN HART	99¾	40	-	-	-	-	-	10	-	149¾	17-18/6	H
A	DUNKELD	100	40½	-	-	-	-	-	10	-	150½	17-22/6	B
B	AFRICAN PRINCE	105	40½	-	-	-	-	-	10	-	155½	10-13/6	B
A	FORT PELLY	651½	1188	348½	32	24½	-	62½	27	328½	2662½	16-25/6	A
A	WILL ROGERS	100	39¾	-	-	32½	-	-	10	-	182¼	11-16/6 and 23/6	A
B	DANIEL FRENCH	650	1178¼	320½	18¾	-	-	62½	10	320	2560¼	16-22/6	H
B	ABNER NASH	643	1162½	353½	38½	-	5	62½	65	312½	2642½	16-25/6	B
B	WILLIAM PATTERSON	666½	1161	345½	38½	-	-	66½	25½	319	2622½	17-26/6	B
B	KAIMATA	533	1160½	-	38½	-	-	62½	17	319	2130½	16-24/6	B
B	CITY OF FLORENCE	730	1173½	410½	48½	-	45	62½	14	321½	2805½	17-26/6	H
B	ZANE GREY	650	1163½	399	17½	-	42½	62½	13	319½	2668	17-23/6	H
B	SAMUEL PARKER	650	1183½	360	17½	-	40	62½	35½	323	2672	17-24/6	H
B	TOWER HILL	730	1181½	282	50	-	-	62½	15	320½	2641½	16-28/6	B
B	FORT GEORGE	661	1202	18	50	-	63	62½	63	323	2442½	16-25/6	A
B	GREYSTOKE CASTLE	546	1129	245½	37	-	-	60	46	217	2280½	17-25/6	A
A	CITY OF EVANSVILLE	100	40	-	-	-	-	-	4	-	144	10-14/6	A
A	TORONTO	100	35¾	-	-	-	-	-	4	-	139¾	17-20/6	A
A	ALGORAB	646	1050	244½	36½	-	-	56	58	187	2278	11-15/6	A
A	NARVIK	120½	35½	-	-	-	-	-	12	-	168	11-16/6	A
B	TRUCKER	260½	1097	261½	95¼	-	-	-	58	192	1972¼	12-28/6	A
B	OCEAN VESPER	680	1000	207	38	-	26	46	8	187	2182	17-25/6	A
B	HARRISON G. OTIS	650½	1204½	335½	43	-	22½	56	23	300	2632½	16-25/6	A
B	THOMAS PICKERING	651	1039½	314	41½	-	18½	56	47	190	2357½	16-25/6	A
B	WILLIAM T. COLEMAN	651	67	255½	43	-	17	56½	39	187	1316	16-26/6	A
B	HERMALIN (Petrol Carrier)	1952	-	-	-	-	-	-	-	100	2052	30/6-5/7	A
B	DIOMED	886	897½	443	96	-	-	107½	140	445½	3015½	17-26/6	A
	TOTAL ...	14709	19709½	5143½	779¾	57½	279½	1067	813¾	5201¾	47761¼		

X PORTS:- A = ALEXANDRIA

B = BEIRUT

H = HAIFA

(111a)

RAIL MOVES — PERSONNEL

PERSONNEL by Rail to SUEZ AREA for embarkation in Troopships.

2nd June – 19th June

Area from	To	No. Special Trains	Personnel conveyed
CANAL	SUEZ	3	1,902
LEVANT	SUEZ and EL SHATT	16	17,250
CANAL	EL SHATT	5	3,781
CAIRO	EL SHATT	1	539
ALEXANDRIA	SUEZ	5	4,134
CANAL	CANAL (Local)	1	999
		31	28,605

27th June – 1st July

CANAL	SUEZ	4	6,495
SUEZ	SUEZ (Local)	7	7,994
		11	14,489

PERSONNEL by Rail to ALEXANDRIA for embarkation to MALTA.

7th / 8th June	CANAL	ALEXANDRIA	4	3,530

388 personnel also conveyed by ordinary service.

PERSONNEL by Rail to SUEZ for embarkation in Troopships for exercise at AQABA.

8th / 9th June	CANAL	SUEZ	4	6,906
	SUEZ	SUEZ	1	703
			5	7,609

PERSONNEL by Rail from LEVANT to ALEXANDRIA for embarkation in M.T. Ships.

1st June – 20th June.

Driving parties after loading vehicles to M.T. Stores Ships at BEIRUT, HAIFA, SUEZ, moved independently by ordinary rail services to ALEXANDRIA area for subsequent embarkation. No separate records available.

SUMMARY OF ROAD MOVES — VEHICLES.

To HAIFA	From DELTA	708	
	Ninth Army	1,168	
	LEVANT	262	2,138
To BEIRUT	From DELTA	623	
	Ninth Army	1,053	
	LEVANT	181	1,857
To ALEXANDRIA	From DELTA	3,623	
	Ninth Army	1	
	LEVANT	306	3,930
		TOTAL:-	7,925

Drivers on the basis of one per vehicle plus 10% spare.

(iv)

Sub-Appendix "D".

EMBARKATION PERSONNEL

"D" Convoy and "D PLUS 3" Convoy

"D" CONVOY.

Ship	Officers	ORs.
TJELBERG	116	1,992
MONARCH OF BERMUDA	147	2,531
DUCHESS OF BEDFORD	197	2,542
WINCHESTER CASTLE	129	862
STRATHNAVER	168	2,812
ORONTES	212	2,899
OTRANTO	143	2,768
SOBIESKI	94	1,183
REINA DEL PACIFICO	154	2,031
DUNERA	114	1,625
DILWARA	164	1,516
DEVONSHIRE	81	1,244
RUYS	130	1,986
BERGENSFJORD	125	2,065
CHRISTIAAN HUYGENS	83	1,511
	2,057	29,567

"D PLUS 3" CONVOY.

Ship	Officers	ORs.
LEOPOLDVILLE	99	1,211
ALMANZORA	65	1,097
ORBITA	90	1,934
ROHNA	112	1,307
RAJULA	39	1,458
KAROA	46	981
TAKLIWA	43	904
AGRA	9	684
KOSIUSKO	53	869
EMPIRE TROOPER	65	1,619
ARONDA	75	1,071
CITY OF CANTERBURY	45	883
	741	14,018

PERSONNEL EMBARKED H.M. SHIPS.

"D" CONVOY

Ship	Officers	ORs.
BULOLO	22	41
KEREN	75	940
PRINCE ALBERT	17	253
ULSTER MONARCH	24	325
	138	1,559

(v)

L.S.Ts. LOADED AT SUEZ AND ALEXANDRIA.

Ship	Officers	ORs.	Vehicles	Loaded at
LST 323	7	112	31	SUEZ and ALEXANDRIA
364	5	171	52	ALEXANDRIA
367	5	157	37	SUEZ and ALEXANDRIA
368	8	148	40	" " "
404	6	150	37	" " "
405	6	160	47	ALEXANDRIA
407	14	190	57	"
409	4	134	43	SUEZ and ALEXANDRIA
411	7	92	24	" " "
413	8	140	42	ALEXANDRIA
414	14	151	41	SUEZ and ALEXANDRIA
415	5	152	48	ALEXANDRIA
416	5	124	56	"
417	4	183	45	"
425	4	143	51	"
	100	2,207	651	

L.C.Ts. LOADED AT BENGHAZI.

17 Inf. Bde.

Ship	Officers	ORs.	Vehicles.
LOT 1	5	65	18
2	5	65	16
3	2	62	20
4	3	60	19
5	2	66	28
6	3	65	24
7	2	68	19
8	3	62	27
9	Was not utilised.	Personnel spread over other LCTs.	
10	4	55	16
11	2	48	17
12	2	59	19
	35	713	240

151 Bde.

Ship	Officers	ORs.	Vehicles.
LOT 101	Was not utilised.	Personnel spread over other LCTs.	
102	2	58	15
103	3	57	17
104	5	57	17
105	5	56	17
106	2	58	16
107	Was not utilised.	Personnel spread over other LCTs.	
108	" "	" "	" "
109	2	58	16
110	2	49	15
111	1	45	13
112	2	40	14
113	1	50	14
114	1	29	13
115	5	31	16
116		29	17
	(sic) 33 (?)	771 (sic)	268 (sic)

231 Bde.

Ship	Officers	ORs.	Vehicles.
LOT 51	2	46	16
52	3	67	14
53	4	42	13
54	3	43	15
55	4	41	16
56	3	41	14
57	2	42	17
58	2	43	17
	23	365	122

15 Inf. Bde.

Ship	Officers	ORs.	Vehicles.
LOT 556	4	82	22
572	2	33	19
586	2	65	13
445	4	67	19
416	2	59	23
307	3	60	20
339	2	36	8
364	ALL RANKS:-	60	15
311		60	17
390		60	17
579		56	15
Old No. 1045	was not utilised.	Personnel spread over other LCTs.	
1046	" "	" "	" "
	19	734	216

(vii)

EMBARKATION PERSONNEL, M.T. STORES SHIPS AND VEHICLES.

"D" CONVOY

Ship	Officers	ORs.	Vehicles	A/Cs.
SHAHJEHAN	6	203	118	
OCEAN GLORY	7	236	109	
THISTLEMUIR	7	184	104	
JOSEPH ALSTON	7	204	134	
FORT LAWRENCE	5	105	98	8
OCEAN VISION	6	223	111	
OCEAN PRIDE	7	209	121	8
OCEAN STRENGTH	8	205	123	
OCEAN VULCAN	8	250	104	
OCEAN HUNTER	11	253	123	24
OCEAN PEACE	11	187	105	11
OCEAN VALLEY	7	175	98	8
BRARN	3	241	160	23
JONATHAN GROUT	13	230	137	
BENJAMIN GOODHUE	3	179	111	
TABANTIA	7	254	120	49
ORANDA	7	239	146	23
GEO. E. CLARKE	5	248	136	30
BARBADOS	5	211	110	
FRANK R. KELLOGG	9	276	182	
JOSEPH G. CANNON	9	232	137	36
LESLIE M. SHAW	6	260	127	
RIO FORT WALLACE	6	285	156	30
O'HENRY	7	175	127	
COLES P. KELLY	7	210	117	
RICHLAND PRINCE	3	191	103	
GEO. E. BADGER	4	191	118	
PIO PICO	4	316		
MATO BROS.	5	205	132	32
POCOHONTAS	3	184	123	
	191	6,537	3,358	292

(viii)

EMBARKATION PERSONNEL M.T. STORES SHIPS AND VEHICLES.

"D PLUS 3" CONVOY.

Ship	Officers	ORs.	Vehicles	M/Cs.
DIOMED	7	206	188	
GREYSTOKE CASTLE	4	170	163	
CITY OF EVANSVILLE	5	146	192	
TORONTO	3	157	174	
ALGORAB	5	178	223	
NARVIK	4	131	172	
TRUCEE	4	209	213	
OCEAN VESPER	2	119	96	48
HARRISON G. OTIS	5	141	120	28
THOMAS PICKERING	4	120	122	37
WM. T. COLEMAN	3	134	125	
ORRA	4	174	163	
DEBRETT	3	214	134	
CHAS. G. CURTIS	8	157	150	10
ABRAHAM LINCOLN	7	171	149	37
RALPH IZARD	4	172	147	21
JOHN HART	4	152	144	43
DUNKELD	6	154	123	34
AFRICAN PRINCE	4	152	132	
FORT PELLY	5	138	120	
WILL ROGERS	8	156	128	12
DANIEL FRENCH	3	135	115	
ABNER NASH	3	130	118	17
WM. PATTERSON	5	143	124	7
KAIMATA	4	185	168	
CITY OF FLORENCE	4	166	153	
ZANE GREY	3	126	113	
SAMUEL PARKER	3	119	107	
TOWER HILL	4	142	121	
FORT GEORGE	2	158	120	
	130	4,655	4,367	294

Appendix E.
Comparative Table of the Different Beach Organisations [274]

COMPARATIVE TABLE OF THE DIFFERENT BEACH GROUP ORGANIZATIONS

	Middle East Type	North Africa Type	United Kingdom Old Type	United Kingdom New Type
Commander Group Headquarters	Colonel Group Headquarters	Colonel Group Headquarters; Detachment Movement Control Group	Lieutenant-Colonel Group Headquarters; Detachment Movement Control Group	Lieutenant-Colonel Group Headquarters; Detachment Movement Control Group (See Note 4).
Artillery	Anti-Aircraft unit H.Q.; Heavy Anti-Aircraft Battery; Light Anti-Aircraft Battery	Detachment Heavy Anti-Aircraftregiment H.Q.; Heavy Anti-Aircraft Battery; Light Anti-Aircraft Battery	One troop Heavy Anti-Aircraft Battery; Light Anti-Aircraft Battery	(See Note 4).
Engineers	Field Company; Mechanical Equipment Detachment	Field Company; Mechanical Equipment Detachment; Beach Depot Section	Field Company; Mechanical Equipment Detachment	Field Company; Mechanical Equipment Detachment.
Signals	Beach Signal Section	Beach Signal Section	Beach Signal Section	Beach Signal Section
Infantry	Infantry Battalion	Detachment Battalion H.Q.; Two Companies Infantry Battalion		Infantry Battalion.
Working Companies	Four Working Companies			
Transportation			Docks Operating Company	Docks Operating Company
Supplies and Transport	H.Q. Field Maintenance Centre; Two General Transport Platoons; Detail Issue Depot; Workshop Platoon General Transport Company	General Transport Company; Petrol Depot Type "C"; Detail Issue Depot	Two General Transport Platoons; Petrol Depot Type "C"; Detail Issue Depot	General Transport Company; Petrol Depot Type "C"; Detail Issue Depot Type "B".
Medical	Beach Group Medical Section	Field Ambulance (less Coy.); Detachment Field Hygiene Section; Detachment Field Surgical Unit	Field Surgical Unit (See Note 1)	Field Dressing Station; Field Surgical Unit; Detachment Field Hygiene Section.
Ordnance	Ordnance Beach Group Detachment	Ordnance Beach Detachment	Ordnance Beach Detachment	Ordnance Detachment.
Royal Electrical and Mechanical Engineers	Beach Group Repairs and Recovery Section	Repair Detachment Recovery Detachment	Tank Repair and Recovery Detachment; Repair Detachment Recovery Detachment	Recovery Detachment.
Provost	Provost Unit	Three Provost Sections	Two Provost Sections	Provost Company (Four Sections)
Labour		Four Pioneer Companies	Three Pioneer Companies	Pioneer Company
Attached Royal Navy	(See Note 2)	Royal Naval Signals	Royal Naval Signals	(See Note 2).
Attached Royal Air Force	(See Note 2)	Royal Naval Beach Party Beach Detachment	Royal Naval Beach Party Beach Detachment	Royal Air Force Beach Flight.

Note 1. Other Medical units found from Divisional resources.

Note 2. Not shown in organization.

Note 3. Amphibian sub-units are not shown in the organization in this operation they were supplementary. A suggested future organization is that two platoons of a General Transport Company should be equipped with amphibians.

Note 4. Not specially included in beach group but on scale one or two Heavy Anti-Aircraft Batteries, one or two Light Anti-Aircraft Batteries, one Mobile Anti-Aircraft Operations room.

Appendix F.

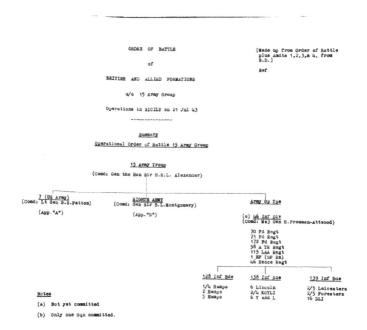

ORDER OF BATTLE

of

BRITISH AND ALLIED FORMATIONS

u/c 15 Army Group

Operations in SICILY on 21 Jul 43

[Made up from Order of Battle plus Amdts 1,2,3,& 4, from S.D.]

Ref.

Summary

Operational Order of Battle 15 Army Group

15 Army Group
(Comd: Gen the Hon Sir H.R.L. Alexander)

7 (US Army)
(Comd: Lt Gen G.S.Patton)
(App."A")

EIGHTH ARMY
(Comd: Gen Sir B.L.Montgomery)
(App."B")

Army Gp Tps

(a) 46 Inf Div
(Comd: Maj Gen H.Freeman-Attwood)

70 Fd Regt
71 Fd Regt
172 Fd Regt
58 A Tk Regt
115 LAA Regt
1 NF (MP Bn)
46 Recce Regt

128 Inf Bde	138 Inf Bde	139 Inf Bde
1/4 Hamps	6 Lincoln	2/5 Leicesters
2 Hamps	2/4 KOYLI	2/5 Foresters
5 Hamps	6 Y and L	16 DLI

Notes

(a) Not yet committed

(b) Only one Sqn committed.

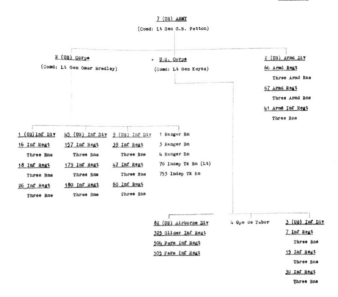

7 (US) ARMY
(Comd: Lt Gen G.S. Patton)

2 (US) Corps
(Comd: Lt Gen Omar Bradley)

* U.S. Corps
(Comd: Lt Gen Keyes)

2 (US) Armd Div
66 Armd Regt
  Three Armd Bns
67 Armd Regt
  Three Armd Bns
41 Armd Inf Regt
  Three Bns

1 (US) Inf Div	45 (US) Inf Div	9 (US) Inf Div	
16 Inf Regt	157 Inf Regt	39 Inf Regt	1 Ranger Bn
Three Bns	Three Bns	Three Bns	3 Ranger Bn
18 Inf Regt	179 Inf Regt	47 Inf Regt	4 Ranger Bn
Three Bns	Three Bns	Three Bns	70 Indep Tk Bn (Lt)
26 Inf Regt	180 Inf Regt	60 Inf Regt	753 Indep Tk Bn
Three Bns	Three Bns	Three Bns	

82 (US) Airborne Div
325 Glider Inf Regt
504 Para Inf Regt
505 Para Inf Regt

4 Gpe de Tabor

3 (US) Inf Div
7 Inf Regt
  Three Bns
15 Inf Regt
  Three Bns
30 Inf Regt
  Three Bns

* Known as Provisional Corps

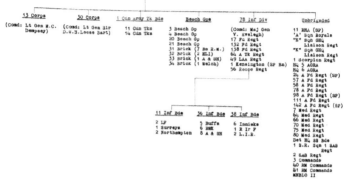

EIGHTH ARMY

(Comd: General Sir B.L.Montgomery)

13 Corps	30 Corps	1 Cdn Army Tk Bde	Beach Gps	78 Inf Div	Unbrigaded
(Comd: Lt Gen M.C. Dempsey)	(Comd: Lt Gen Sir O.W.H.Leese Bart)	11 Cdn Tks 14 Cdn Tks	3 Beach Gp 4 Beach Gp 20 Beach Gp 21 Beach Gp 31 Brick (7 Bn R.M.) 32 Brick (2 HLI) 33 Brick (1 A & SH) 34 Brick (1 Welch)	(Comd: Maj Gen V. Eveleigh) 17 Fd Regt 132 Fd Regt 138 Fd Regt 64 A Tk Regt 49 LAA Regt 1 Kensington (SP Bn) 56 Recce Regt	11 RHA (SP) 'A' Sqn Royals "H" Sqn GHQ Liaison Regt "K" Sqn GHQ Liaison Regt 1 Scorpion Regt HQ 5 AGRA HQ 6 AGRA 24 A Fd Regt (SP) 57 A Fd Regt 58 A Fd Regt 78 A Fd Regt 98 A Fd Regt (SP) 111 A Fd Regt 142 A Fd Regt (SP) 7 Med Regt 64 Med Regt 66 Med Regt 70 Med Regt 75 Med Regt 80 Med Regt Det HQ SS Bde 1 S.R. Sqn 1 SAS Regt 2 SAS Regt 3 Commando 40 RM Commando 41 RM Commando MNBLO II

11 Inf Bde	36 Inf Bde	38 Inf Bde
2 LF 1 Surreys 2 Northampton	5 Buffs 6 RWK 8 A & SH	6 Innisks 1 R Ir F 2 L.I.R.

139

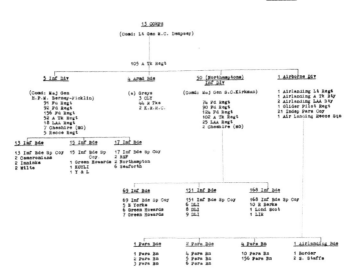

13 CORPS

(Comd: Lt Gen M.C. Dempsey)

105 A Tk Regt

5 Inf Div

(Comd: Maj Gen
H.P.M. Berney-Ficklin)
91 Fd Regt
92 Fd Regt
156 Fd Regt
52 A Tk Regt
18 LAA Regt
7 Cheshire (MG)
5 Recce Regt

4 Armd Bde

(a) Greys
3 CLY
44 R Tks
2 K.R.R.C.

**50 (Northamptons)
Inf Div**

(Comd: Maj Gen S.C.Kirkman)
74 Fd Regt
90 Fd Regt
124 Fd Regt
102 A Tk Regt
25 LAA Regt
2 Cheshire (MG)

1 Airborne Div

1 Airlanding Lt Regt
1 Airlanding A Tk Bty
2 Airlanding LAA Bty
1 Glider Pilot Regt
21 Indep Para Coy
1 Air Landing Recce Sqn

13 Inf Bde

13 Inf Bde Sp Coy
2 Cameronians
2 Inniks
2 Wilts

15 Inf Bde

15 Inf Bde Sp
Coy.
1 Green Howards
1 KOYLI
1 Y & L

17 Inf Bde

17 Inf Bde Sp Coy
2 RSF
2 Northampton
6 Seaforth

69 Inf Bde

69 Inf Bde Sp Coy
5 E Yorks
6 Green Howards
7 Green Howards

151 Inf Bde

151 Inf Bde Sp Coy
6 DLI
8 DLI
9 DLI

168 Inf Bde

168 Inf Bde Sp Coy
10 R Berks
1 Lond Scot
1 LIR

1 Para Bde

1 Para Bn
2 Para Bn
3 Para Bn

2 Para Bde

4 Para Bn
5 Para Bn
6 Para Bn

4 Para Bn

10 Para Bn
156 Para Bn

1 Airlanding Bde

1 Border
2 S. Staffs

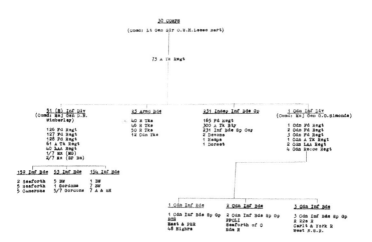

30 CORPS

(Comd: Lt Gen Sir O.W.H.Leese Bart)

73 A Tk Regt

51 (H) Inf Div
(Comd: Maj Gen D.N. Wimberley)

126 Fd Regt
127 Fd Regt
128 Fd Regt
61 A Tk Regt
40 LAA Regt
1/7 Mx (MG)
2/7 Mx (SP Bn)

152 Inf Bde

2 Seaforth
5 Seaforth
5 Camerons

53 Inf Bde

5 BW
1 Gordons
5/7 Gordons

154 Inf Bde

1 BW
7 BW
7 A & sH

23 Armd Bde

40 R Tks
46 R Tks
50 R Tks
12 Cdn Tks

231 Indep Inf Bde Gp

165 Fd Regt
300 A Tk Bty
231 Inf Bde Sp Coy
2 Devons
1 Hamps
1 Dorset

1 Cdn Inf Div (Comd: Maj Gen G.G.Simonds)

1 Cdn Fd Regt
2 Cdn Fd Regt
3 Cdn Fd Regt
1 Cdn A Tk Regt
2 Cdn LAA Regt
4 Cdn Recce Regt

1 Cdn Inf Bde

1 Cdn Inf Bde Sp Gp
RCR
Hast & PER
48 Highrs

2 Cdn Inf Bde

2 Cdn Inf Bde Sp Gp
PPCLI
Seaforth of C
Edm R

3 Cdn Inf Bde

3 Cdn Inf Bde Sp Gp
R 22e R
Carlt & York R
West N.S.R.

Appendix G.
103 Beach Sub-Area D-day to D+13
Summary of Position on Bark Beaches at 1700hrs daily [276]

APPENDIX "A"

103 BEACH SUB-AREA

Summary of position on BARK beaches at 1700 hours daily

	(A) Number of personnel landed	(B) Number of ships working and ETC	(C) Number of ships waiting to work	(D) Number of ships completed	(E) Number of vehicles landed	(F) Tonnage of stores landed on to beaches	(G) Tonnage of stores from beaches to dumps	(H) Tonnages issued from dumps	(I) Number of Landing Craft by types
D	17,670	20	5	11	450	160	?		DUKWS 54 LCT 10 LCM 50
D+1	1,200	15	...	8	700	1,200	?	?	.. 66 .. 16 .. 49
D+2	1,786	12	...	6	690	1,500	900	?	.. 81 .. 16 .. 45
D+3	7,700	24	...	7	380	1,700	1,120	?	.. 80 .. 16 .. 40
D+4	1,200	21	...	...	413	2,259	2,375	?	.. 94 .. 16 .. 40
D+5	950	16	...	5	513	1,635	1,230	?	.. 156 .. 16 .. 40
D+6	440	12	...	4	225	2,218	2,160	?	.. 145 .. 15 .. 37
D+7	100	8	...	...	91	3,461	2,455	340	.. 128 .. 14 .. 43
D+8	80	8	...	...	50	4,177	3,265	540	.. 123 .. 14 .. 43
D+9	450	8	...	...	386	3,625	3,613	740	.. 125 .. 14 .. 43
D+10	400	8	...	...	352	4,914	3,527	1,200	.. 125 .. 14 .. 43
D+11	160	7	...	1	153	5,181	3,807	?	.. 125 .. 14 .. 43
D+12	...	4	...	3		3,535	?	?	.. 125 .. 14 .. 43
D+13	2	4	...	4	1	2,682	?	?	.. 125 .. 14 .. 43
TOTAL	32,148	...	...	...	4,364	38,177	...		

Notes:—

1 *Number of ships working:—*

Ships working from D to D+3 were the assault convoy. On D+3, the follow-up convoy arrived. In addition L.S.T. and L.C.T. from MALTA and SOUSSE were being discharged. This explains why large numbers of vehicles were still being landed on D+9 and D+10.

2 *Columns (F) and (G).*

The daily receipts into the dumps (Column (G)) did not correspond to the daily tonnages landed on the beaches (Column (F)) because some of the stores were loaded direct into 3rd line transport or loaded to the railway station without passing through the dumps. Also from D+10 onwards, in order that sailing of the convoy should not be delayed, stores were dumped on to the beaches and not into the proper depots.

3. The rate of issue from dumps on 17 and 18 July represent the average daily delivery by 3rd line transport to stock the F.M.C. at PALAZZALO, i.e., an average lift of 450 tons for a "scratch" 3rd line of 5 platoons.

The rise in tonnage on 19 and 20 July is explained by the despatch by rail of about 450 tons of stores daily from PACHINO and MARZAMEMI to SYRACUSE railhead.

4 The average daily maintenance requirements of 30 Corps exclusive of Air Force requirements worked out at about 650 tons whereas the receipts into the dumps from D+5 onwards averaged about 2,000 tons. Therefore, the rate of build-up was 1,350 tons per day or approximately double the consumption rate. This is unnecessarily high and explains why the depots were unable to handle the tonnage

(142860)

ii

4 BEACH GROUP

Vehicles and stores discharged at BARK SOUTH daily

Date	Vehicles	Tonnage discharged	Tonnage received into dump
D + 4	340	1,014	840
D + 5	339	1,485	1,080
D + 6	201	1,638	1,580
D + 7	91	2,220	1,459
D + 8	50	2,752	1,840
D + 9	386	2,805	1,444
D + 10	352	4,049	2,197
D + 11	153	4,376	2,500
D + 12		2,635	?
D + 13		1,782	?

Note

1. *Average lighterage available for discharge was* :—

DUKWS	120
Landing Craft (Mechanized)	30
Landing Craft (Tank)	9

2. *Average labour available* —On the average the following labour was available :—

(i) *On the beach*—

Pioneers	250
Reinforcements	400
Prisoners of War	700

(ii) *In the dumps*—Two Pioneer Companies were normally employed.

3. *Average Transport available* :—10 × 3-ton lorries.

4 BEACH GROUP

Receipts and issues from dumps over average period of 4 days D + 6 to D + 9 inclusive

Nature of Stores	Date	Held at 1700 hours previous day	Received during last 24 hours	Issued during last 24 hours	Balance remaining	Remark.
Supplies	17/7	22	404	67	359	
	18/7	359	445	25	779	
	19/7	779	67	174	672	
	20/7	946	623	284	1,285	
Water	17/7	100	56	24	132	
	18/7	132	25	20	190	
	19/7	137	74	21	190	
	20/7*					*Tonnage included in Supplies tonnage.
Petrol, Oil and Lubricants	17/7	1,626	562	162	2,026	
	18/7	2.026	493	139	2,380	
	19/7	2,382	238	138	2,482	
	20/7	2,482	644	87	3,039	
Ammunition	17/7	942	247	33	1,156	
	18/7	1,256	598	56	1,698	
	19/7	1,698	750	118	2,330	
	20/7	2,330	568	129	2,769	
Ordnance Stores	17/7	260	143	2	401	
	18/7	401	124	28	497	
	19/7	497	85	30	552	
	20/7	552	68	6	614	
Royal Engineer Stores	17/7	315	45		360	
	18/7	360	360†		720	†Inclusive 200 tons not previously accounted for
	19/7	720	210	50	880	
	20/7	880	220	20	1,100	

Appendix H.
H.Q. 15 Army Group
Weekly Administrative Review, August 1943 [277]

WEEKLY ADMINISTRATIVE REVIEW sent by H.Q. 15 ARMY GROUP to A.F.H.Q.

ADMINISTRATIVE SUMMARY AS AT 1200 hours: EIGHTH ARMY – SICILY

AUGUST, 1943.

PORTS and BEACHES Discharges	Stocks	General Notes
SYRACUSE 30 July. Stores 5148 tons Vehicles 449 The highest total so far. AUGUSTA average 1500 tons per day.	4 August. P.O.L. 13 Corps ..... 250 miles 30 Corps ..... 150 " Canadian Div. ..... 200 " Army Depôts ..... 22,679 tons Supplies 13 Corps ..... 2 days 30 Corps ..... 3 days (78 Div. ..... 2 days) Army Depôts ..... 9½ days for Force. Ammunition 2 August: Stocks satisfactory except 5.5-in., but shortage not causing concern.	CATANIA captured 5 August. Intention to use port for embarkation and not the discharge of maintenance convoys. ACIP beaches closed 5 August. TOTAL discharges ports and beaches to 4 August: 142,608 tons. First train of 200 tons capacity for 13 Corps due to arrive LENTINI 0800 hours 7 August. Additional to 3 pack trains, each 250 tons, to SCORDIA for 30 Corps. General administrative situation of 15 Army Group satisfactory.
SYRACUSE 12/8 Stores 5592 tons Vehicles 748 13/8 Stores 5076 tons Vehicles 155 AUGUSTA 12/8 Stores 1104 tons Vehicles 661 13/8 Stores 1100 tons Vehicles 216	12 August. P.O.L. 13 Corps ..... 250 miles Canadian Div. 150 " 30 Corps ..... 150 " 78 Div. ..... 200 " Supplies 13 Corps ..... 2 days Canadian Div. 4 " 30 Corps ..... 3 " 51 Div. ..... 2 " 78 Div. ..... 4 " Ammunition Stocks adequate on 7 August; expenditure reduced as pursuit proceeds.	Captured stocks of P.O.L. exceed 500,000 gls. but require analysis. CATANIA. Damage mainly consists of damaged bollards. One berth is blocked by sunken train and one by a sunken ship alongside. Span of railway viaduct broken; expect to repair by 16/17 Aug. when clearance capacity from docks estimated at 600 tons per day. 30 locomotives and approximately 250 wagons captured in working order. Proposed use of port as follows: Hards are being prepared for 16 L.S.T. and 16 L.C.T.; not intended to use port for discharge at present. 13 Corps withdrawn from active operations and maintained through F.M.C. LENTINI. Opening of Railhead MOTTA was delayed by enemy air attack; anticipated date now 16 Aug. General administrative situation satisfactory.

TOTAL for week ending 19 August.
Stores
TONS Personnel Vehs.
30,105 296 446
6,399 3,649 1782
D+45 days convoy from M.E. 21 August; ships allotted as follows:-
3 M.T./stores ships
3 M.T. ships
2 cased POL carriers
1 Mule ship
4 personnel ships.
	P.O.L.
	13 Corps ..... 200 miles
	30 Corps ..... 230 "
	51 Div. ..... 150 "
	23 Armd Bde ..... 160 "
	Supplies
	13 Corps ..... 2 days
	30 Corps ..... 2 "
	Army Depôts .... 8½ days for force.
	P.O.L.
	Army Depôts ..... 22,662 tons = 36 days at average rate of issues.
	Ammunition P.N.R.
	25 pdr. H.E. 1,139
	4.5-in. 307
	5.5-in. 374
	3.7 A.A. 578
	40 mm. 1,165
		CATANIA: A proportion of Air Corps bombs for GERBINI airfields to be unloaded at CATANIA.
		Railway situation for week ending 15 August.
		                        Standard Narrow
		Track in use and available 193 mls 91 mls
		Engines available including under repair 35 9
		Freight rolling stock including under repair .. 324 78
		Coaching stock 22 23
		Diesel railcars ..... 2 –
		Coal consumed ..... 301 tons 14 tons
		Stock in hand in WEEKS .. 3 5
		    Only one train running daily on narrow gauge. Negotiations proceeding for AMGOT to take over narrow gauge railway SYRACUSE – VIZZINI – RAGUSA. 80 ft. gap to be bridged in viaduct at CATANIA, damage caused by Allied bombing.
		New boundary fixed between 7(U.S.) and Eighth Armies. Divisions moving to concentration areas to rest and refit.
		General administrative situation satisfactory.

(1)

PORTS and BEACHES Discharges			

Week ending 26/8.

	Stores TONS	Personnel	Vehs.
SYRACUSE	19,700	643	1325
AUGUSTA	1,533	10,454	904
CATANIA	4,968	168	-

Stocks

Army dumps 1800 hrs. 22/8.

P.O.L. 24,952 tons = 31 days' average daily issues.

Supplies 5 days average daily issues.

Ammunition

	F.B.ds.
25 pdr. H.E.	1,493
4.5-in.	458
5.5-in.	463
3.7-in. A.A.	561
40 mm. A.A.	1,230

BAYTOWN Dumps. at 23 August.

Supplies	1,731 tons
P.O.L.	4,609 "
Ammunition	6,380 "
Ord. stores	357
	13,077 tons

Eighth Army Reserve (MALTA)

	Awaiting Shipment	Awaiting Disposal
	T O N S	
Supplies	3,300	-
P.O.L.	NIL	1,946
Ammunition	1,875	1,700

(ii)

General Notes

Evacuation - satisfactory.

Total casualties (incl. sick) evacuated to 25 August ... 15,890

Casualties evacuated 24 July to 23 August. Air: 38% Sea: 62%

P.W. evacuated to 25 August 25,195

GENERAL.

(i) 2 & 3 C.R.Us. loaded BIZERTA for SICILY 23 August.

(ii) s.s. LETITIA sailed for AUGUSTA 20 August with reinforcements.

	Officers	O.Rs.
British ...	55	800
Canadian ...	115	1,286

(iii) Cases of malaria confirmed and clinical 1 to 21 August: 6,361.

The following is a brief survey of the Adm. situation as seen by H.Q. 15 Army Group on 28 August.

1. **SEVENTH ARMY.** There are considerable stocks of all classes in Seventh Army area, but there are certain shortages which are being rectified - PALERMO is being set up as the main depot

(a) for maintenance of Seventh Army in SICILY;

(b) as a reserve for shipment to 5 Army in PANTALOON.

Railways and roads are being repaired as rapidly as the resources available permit. Railheads are now in operation at LICATA, TRAPANI, CINISI, TERMINI IMERESE and CEFALU. The railway LICATA to GERBINI area is being used for the movement of air supplies from southern dumps to GERBINI Airfields, but there is still a gap in this railway between GERBINI and CATANIA.

2. **EIGHTH ARMY.** Stocks in hand in Army Depots under FORTBASE are satisfactory. The main problems confronting Eighth Army at the present moment are:-

(a) The mounting and maintenance preparations for BAYTOWN.

(b) The maintenance of Air Forces, supplies for which are now beginning to arrive in eastern Sicilian ports.

Malaria figures tend to show an increase but in other respects the health of the Army appears satisfactory.

3. **A.M.G.O.T.** Supplies for A.M.G.O.T. are reported satisfactory. The main difficulties are distribution and shortage of transport.

General Administrative situation satisfactory.

Bibliography

A: **Primary Sources, Unpublished**

(i) Official Documents

The National Archives (TNA), Kew, London

ADM Series - Records created or inherited by the Admiralty, Naval Forces, Coastguard, and related bodies:

ADM 199/2509: Report of Eastern Task Force (Vice Admiral Ramsay)

ADM 199/2510: Report of Western Task Force (Vice Admiral Hewitt)

ADM 199/2515: Mounting the Expedition in the Eastern Mediterranean (Admiral Cunningham)

AIR Series - Records created or inherited by the Air Ministry, the Royal Air Force, and related bodies:

AIR 8/1344: Operation Husky

AIR 23/3342: History of AFHQ Part I

AIR 23/3343: History of AFHQ Part II section I

AIR 23/3344: History of AFHQ Part II Section II

AIR 23/3345: History of AFHQ Part II Section II

AIR 23/3346: History of AFHQ Part II section IV

AIR 23/5759: Invasion of Sicily: planning

AIR 23/6216: R.A.F. Mediterranean Review No. 4

AIR 23/6327: Operation 'Husky': map of Sicily

AIR 23/6564: Operation Torch: report on impressions gained from the assault stage

CAB Series - Records of the Cabinet Office:

CAB 44/123: Section IV, chapter A: outline plan for the invasion of Sicily, operation 'Husky', by Major F. Jones

CAB 44/124: Section IV, chapters B and C; amphibious operations, 1943 July 9-10; the securing of the bridgehead, 1943 July 11-12, by Major F. Jones

CAB 44/125: Section IV, chapter D: advance to the "Etna Line", 1943 July 14-21, by Major F. Jones

CAB 44/164: Section VI, chapter K: North Africa: planning, development and maintenance 1942 Nov. 8-1943 May 31, by Brigadier W. P. Pessell

CAB 44/165: Section VI, chapter L: Sicily; planning and maintenance 1943, by Brigadier W. P. Pessell

CAB 80/68: CAB 80. Memoranda (O) Nos. 101-200

CAB 106/637 Sicily: reports on operation Husky, the invasion of Sicily 1943 July, by Admiral of the Fleet Sir Andrew B. Cunningham, Commander-in-Chief, Mediterranean and Vice-Admiral B. H. Ramsay, Commander Eastern Task Force

CAB 106/705: Sicily: despatch on the invasion 1943 July, by Admiral of the Fleet Sir Andrew B. Cunningham, Commander-in-Chief, Mediterranean

DEFE Series – Records of the Ministry of Defence

DEFE 2/1412: Newspaper Coverage of Sicily Invasion

WO Series - Records created or inherited by the War Office, Armed Forces, Judge Advocate General, and related bodies:

WO 106/3862: Operation Husky: Force 141: planning instructions

WO 106/3866: Operation Husky: Shipping

WO 106/3875: Husky: Training

WO 106/3886: The Conquest of Sicily: despatch by Field Marshal Alexander

WO 106/5823: Plans for Operation Husky: messages from General Montgomery

WO 107/135: Husky: Lessons from operation: report on beach maintenance in Sicily

WO 201/658: Husky: 30 Corps beach landing maps

WO 201/660: Husky: 8th Army first report and lessons

WO 204/517: Operation Husky: memoranda on accommodation, logistics and planning

WO 204/520: Operation Husky: maintenance and administration: minutes of meetings

WO 204/1406: Operation Husky: joint service exercises in preparation

WO 204/1409: Operation Husky: map photographs

WO 204/1410: Operation Husky: narrative

WO 204/1906: Tactical lessons from the Sicilian campaign

WO 204/4690 Logistical planning and reference data. Operation Husky: controlled stores: policy

WO 204/6021: Includes COHQ Notes on U.S. Planning and Assault Phases of Operation Husky - by a British Military Observer

WO 204/6898: Lessons learned from the Sicilian campaign: A.F.H.Q Training Memorandum

WO 204/6982: Operation Husky: Beach Groups and maintenance Bricks organisation

WO 204/7525: Lessons learned from training exercises

WO 204/7541: Report by Chief Engineer, 15 Army Group

WO 204/7546: Fortbase: administrative lessons learned

WO 252/885: Sicily: beaches and harbours

WO 252/1199: Beach intelligence reports: Operation HUSKY

(ii) Private Papers

Churchill College Cambridge, United Kingdom

GBR/0014/ROSK: Papers of Captain S W Roskill, naval Historian, World War II

GBR/0014/RMSY: Papers of Admiral Sir Bertram Home

Imperial War Museum, United Kingdom

12979: Private papers of Lieutenant General Charles Gairdner

1838: Correspondence between General Montgomery and Sir Frank Simpson

Liddell Hart Centre for Military Archives (King's College, London)

GB0099 KCLMA Abraham: Papers of Major General Sir W. E. V. Abraham

GB0099 KCMLA Alanbrooke 6/1/1: Copy of SYMBOL conference proceedings

GB0099 KCMLA Alanbrooke 6/1/2: Copy of Trident and Algiers conference proceedings

GB0099 KCMLA Alanbrooke 6/12/17: Correspondence Alexander/Alanbrooke

GB0099 KCMLA Alanbrooke 6/2/22: Correspondence Montgomery/Alanbrooke up to May 1943

GB0099 KCMLA Alanbrooke 6/2/23: Correspondence Montgomery/Alanbrooke from May – December 1943

GB0099 KCMLA Alanbrooke 6/2/46: Correspondence Maitland-Wilson/Alanbrooke

GB0099 KCMLA Alanbrooke 6/7/4: Extensive notes taken by Brigadier E. I. C Jacob at Operation SYMBOL conference

GB0099 KCLMA Burton: Papers of Capt. John George Burton (Husky War Diary 1, 5, 6, 9, 10)

GB0099 KCLMA Clarke E H: Memoir of Lieutenant Colonel E. H. Clarke

GB0099 Davidson 4/2/2: Papers of Major General Francis Henry Norman Davidson - Sicily assault maps

GB0099 KCMLA Gale 2/1-13: Papers of Lieutenant General

Sir Humfrey Myddleton Gale (War diaries December 1942 - December 1943)

GB0099 KCMLA Laycock 5/22, 5/23, 6/22: Papers of Major General Sir Robert Laycock

GB0099 KCMLA Liddell Hart 11/1943/57: Personal views on Husky, Montgomery

GB0099 KCMLA Salmon, H M 1/1, 1/6, 1/7, 2/1: Papers of Colonel H. M. Salmon

B: Primary Sources, Published

(i) Published Diaries, Letters and Memoirs

Bradley, Omar, and Clay Blair, *A General's Life* (New York: Simon and Schuster, 1983)

Butcher, Harry C., *My Three Years with Eisenhower* (New York: Simon & Schuster, 1946)

Eisenhower, Dwight D., *Crusade in Europe* (London: Heinemann, 1948)

Heavey, William F., *Down Ramp: The Story of the Army Amphibian Engineers* (Washington DC: Infantry Journal Press, 1947)

Huie, William Bradford, *Can Do! The Story of the Seabees* (New York: American Book-Stratford Press, 1944)

Kesselring, Albert, *The Memoirs of Field-Marshall Kesselring* (London: William Kimber, 1953)

Morgan, Frederick, *Peace and War: A Soldier's Life* (London: Hodder and Stoughton, 1961)

Pyle, Ernie, *Brave Men* (Lincoln, University of Nebraska

Press, 2001)

Tedder, Arthur, *With Prejudice: The World War II Memoirs of Marshall of the Air Force Lord Tedder* (London: Cassell, 1966)

Truscott, Lt General L.K., *Command Missions: A Personal Story* (New York: E.P. Dutton, 1954)

Von Moltke, Helmuth Graf, and Daniel J. Hughes, *Moltke on the Art of War: Selected Writings* (New York: Random House, 1993)

White, Nathan W., *From Fedala to Berchtesgaden: A History of the Seventh United States Infantry in World War II* (Brockton M.A.: Keystone, 1947)

Wolfe, Martin, *Green Light! A Troop Carrier Squadron's War from Normandy to the Rhine* (Washington DC: University of Pennsylvania Press, 1989)

C: Secondary Sources

(i)   Books

Atkinson, Rick, *The Day of Battle: The War in Sicily and Italy, 1943-44* (London: Abacus, 2007; repr. 2014)

Ballantine, Duncan S., *U.S. Naval Logistics in the Second World War* (Newport R.I.: Naval War College Press, 1998)

Behrens, C. B. A., *Merchant Shipping and the Demands of War* (London: Her Majesty's Stationery Office, 1978)

Birtle, Andrew J., *The US Army Campaigns of World War II: Sicily* (Washington DC: U.S. Army Center of Military History, 1993)

Blackwell, Ian, *The Battle for Sicily: Stepping Stone to*

Victory (Barnsley: Pen and Sword, 2008)

Blumenson, Martin, *Sicily: Whose Victory?* (New York: Ballantine, 1968)

Breuer, William B., *Drop Zone Sicily: Allied Airborne Strike, July 1943* (Novato, Calif.: Presidio Press, 1983: repr. 1997)

Churchill, Winston S., *The River War - An Historical Account of the Reconquest of the Soudan, Volume I* (London: Longmans, Green and Co., 1899)

Craven, F. W., and J. L. Cate, *The Army Air Forces in World War II Volume 2 Europe: Torch to Pointblank, August 1942 to December 1943* (Chicago: University of Chicago Press, 1949)

D'Este, Carlo, *Bitter Victory: The Battle for Sicily, 1943* (New York: William Collins Sons and Co. Ltd., 1988: repr. 2008)

Fergusson, Bernard, *The Watery Maze: The Story of Combined Operations* (London: Collins, 1961)

Ford, Ken, *Assault on Sicily: Monty and Patton at War* (Stroud: Sutton Publishing, 2007)

Garland, Albert N., and Howard McGaw Smyth, *United States Army in World War II: The Mediterranean Theatre of Operations: Sicily and the Surrender of Italy* (Washington: Center of Military History, 1965)

Grehan, John, and Martin Mace, *The War in Italy 1943-1944: Despatches from the Front* (Barnsley: Pen & Sword, 2014)

Gooderson, Ian, *A Hard Way to Make a War: The Allied Campaign in Italy in the Second World War* (London:

Conway, 2008)

Gropman Alan L., *The Big 'L': American Logistics in World War II* (Washington DC: National Defense University Press, 1997)

Howard, Michael, *Grand Strategy Volume IV August 1942 - September 1943* (London, Her Majesty's Stationery Office, 1972)

Kent, Ron, *First In! Parachute Pathfinder Company* (London: Batsford, 1979)

Jones, Matthew, *Britain, the United States and the Mediterranean War, 1942-44* (London: Macmillan Press, 1996)

Lewis, Norman, *The Honoured Society: The Sicilian Mafia Observed* (London: William Collins, 1962; repr. 2003)

Linklater, Eric *The Campaign in Italy* (London: His Majesty's Stationery Office, 1951)

Macintyre, Ben, *Agent Zigzag & Operation Mincemeat* (London: Bloomsbury, 2010)

Matloff, Maurice, *Strategic Planning for Coalition Warfare, 1943-1944* (Washington: Center of Military History United States Army, 1959)

Mitcham, Samuel W. Jr., and Friedrich von Stauffenberg, *The Battle of Sicily: How the Allies Lost Their Chance for Total Victory* (New York: Orion Books, 1991)

Molony, C. J. C., *The Mediterranean and Middle East Volume V: The Campaign in Sicily 1943* (Uckfield: The Naval & Military Press, 1973)

Morison, Samuel Eliot, *History of United States Naval*

Operations in World War II: Sicily-Salerno-Anzio January 1943 - June 1944 (Boston: Little, Brown, 1954)

Nicholson, G. W. L., *Official History of the Canadian Army in the Second World War: Volume II, The Canadians in Italy 1943-45* (Ottowa: Edmond Cloutier, 1956)

Pack, S. W. C., *Operation Husky: The Allied Invasion of Sicily* (Newton Abbot: David & Charles, 1977)

Perret, Geoffrey, *Eisenhower* (New York: Random House, 1999)

Pond, Hugh, *Sicily* (London: William Kimber, 1962)

Roskill, S. W., *The War at Sea 1939-1945 Volume III: The Offensive* (Uckfield: The Naval & Military Press, 1960)

Stacey, C. P., *The Canadian Army 1939-1945* (Ottowa: Edmond Cloutier, 1948)

Van Creveld, Martin, *Supplying War: Logistics from Wallenstein to Patton* (Cambridge: Cambridge University Press, 1977; repr. 2004)

Wallace, Robert, *The Italian Campaign* (New York: Time-Life Books, 1978)

Whiting, Charles, *Slaughter over Sicily* (London: Leo Cooper, 1992)

Willard, James, *General George S. Patton, Jr: Men Under Mars* (New York: Dodd, Mead & Company, 1946)

Zaloga, Steven J., *Sicily 1943 The Debut of Allied Joint Operations* (Oxford: Osprey, 2015)

Zuehlke, Mark, *Operation Husky: The Canadian Invasion of Sicily, July 10-August 7, 1943* (Vancouver: Douglas &

MacIntyre, 2008)

(ii) Unpublished Theses

Barnhart, Major Barton V., 'The Great Escape: An Analysis of Allied Actions Leading to the Axis Evacuation of Sicily in World War II' (unpublished doctoral thesis, School of Advanced Military Studies, Fort Leavenworth, Kansas, 1988)

Cote, Lieutenant Colonel Stephen R., 'Operation Husky: A Critical Analysis' (unpublished doctoral thesis, Naval War College, Newport, R.I., 2001)

Leppard, Christine, 'Fighting as Colony? 1st Canadian Corps in Italy, 1943-1945' (unpublished doctoral thesis, University of Calgary, 2013)

McKenzie, Major Geoffrey M., 'Operation Husky: Seeking an Operational Approach to Decisive Victory' (unpublished doctoral thesis, School of Advanced Military Studies, Fort Leavenworth, Kansas, 2014)

Prescott, Lieutenant Colonel James E., 'What Operational Level of War Lesson can be Learned from the Allied Invasion of Sicily' (unpublished doctoral thesis, Naval War College, Newport, R.I., 1994)

Smith, General Holland M., 'The Development of Amphibious Tactics in the US Navy' (unpublished doctoral thesis, History and Museums Division HQ, US Marine Corps, Washington D.C., 1992)

Stone, Trevor, 'Many Roads, Many Bridges: An analysis of the logistical support of the British 2nd Tactical Air Force during the Allied advance from Normandy 1944-1945' (unpublished doctoral thesis, University of Buckingham, 2019)

Warren, Dr. John C., 'Airborne Missions in the Mediterranean 1942-1945' (unpublished doctoral thesis, USAF Historical Division, Maxwell, Al., 1955)

Wisbith, Thomas, 'Allied Force Headquarters during the North African Campaign: A Study of Allied Integrated Multi-National Command Organization from August 1942 – May 1943' (unpublished doctoral thesis, Ohio State University, 2018)

(iii) Conference Paper or Lecture
David, Saul, 'The Force: The First Special Service and the Capture of Monte la Difensa, December 1943', lecture given at the Caledonian Club, London, 29 October 2018

Walker, Air Marshal Dr. David, 'Portal as Supreme Air Commander', lecture given at the Caledonian Club, London, 10 December 2018

(iv) Online Sources

The Website of the Government of Canada
Canadian Military Headquarters (CMHQ) Reports 1940-1948

CMHQ Report #126: Canadian Operations in Sicily, July - August 1943. Part I: The Preliminaries of OPERATION HUSKY (The Assault on Sicily)

CMHQ Report #127, Canadian Operations in Sicily, July - August 1943. Part II: The Execution of the operation by 1 Cdn Inf Div, Section 1, The Assault and Initial Penetration Inland

CMHQ Report #136, Canadian Operations in Sicily, July - August 1943. Part II: The Execution of the Operation by 1 Cdn Inf Div. Section 3: Special Aspects of the Sicilian Campaign

(v) Internet

Leppard, Christine, 'Documenting the D-Day Dodgers: Canadian Field Historians in the Italian Campaign, 1943-1945', Canadian Military History: Vol. 18: Iss. 3, Article 3.

[1] Arthur Tedder, *With Prejudice: The World War II Memoirs of Marshall of the Air Force Lord Tedder* (London: Cassell, 1966), p. 431. Cable from Montgomery to Alanbrooke, 19 April 1943.

[2] Albert N. Garland and Howard McGaw Smyth, *United States Army in World War II: The Mediterranean Theatre of Operations: Sicily and the Surrender of Italy* (Washington: Center of Military History, 1965), p. 88

[3] Operation Overlord was the codename for the Battle of Normandy, the Allied operation that launched the successful invasion of northern France, on 6 June 1944.

[4] Arthur Tedder, *With Prejudice: The World War II Memoirs of Marshall of the Air Force Lord Tedder* (London: Cassell, 1966), p. 431. Cable from Montgomery to Alanbrooke, 19 April 1943.

ENDNOTES

[5] D-day was the designation traditionally used for the date of any important military operation and was set as 10 July 1943 for Operation Husky. The day before 10 July 1943 was referred to as D-1 and the days after as D+1, D+2 and so on. H-hour was the hour at which any military operation was to begin. H-hour for Operation Husky was set at 0245hrs on 10 July 1943.

[6] Winston S. Churchill, *The River War: An Historical Account of the Reconquest of the Soudan* (London: Longmans, Green and Co., 1899), I, 275-276.

[7] London, The National Archives (TNA), WO 106/3886, 'The Conquest of Sicily': despatch by Field Marshall Alexander. Plan for Operation 'Husky', Joint Planning Staff, London Annexes I and II, pp. 36-69. The Symbol conference was held in Casablanca from 14 to 24 January 1943. President Roosevelt and Prime Minister Churchill, with their respective entourages, met to plan the Allied European strategy for the next phase of the Second World War. Premier Joseph Stalin declined an invitation to attend, citing the ongoing Battle of Stalingrad as requiring his presence in the Soviet Union.

[8] TNA, WO 106/3886, 'The Conquest of Sicily': despatch by Field Marshall Alexander. Force 141 Planning Instruction No. 1, pp. 30-32.

[9] The Axis powers formally took their name from the Tripartite Pact which was signed by Germany, Italy and Japan in Berlin on 27 September 1940. Axis forces in North Africa and in Sicily comprised German and Italian forces.

[10] The Trident conference was held in Washington from 12 to 25 May 1943. President Roosevelt and Prime Minister Churchill met to discuss plans for the Allied invasion of Sicily, the date for invading Normandy and the progress of the Pacific war.

[11] Molony, *The Mediterranean and Middle East,* V, 30. Other commentators cite a larger number of vessels in the armada. In his after-action report on Husky (TNA, ADM 199/2510, Report of Western Task Force, Part I, p. 1.), Admiral Hewitt, who commanded the United States Western Naval Task Force, said the Allied fleet contained 'over 3200 ships, crafts, and boats'. It is possible he is including the assault landing craft in his total which would have travelled on larger ships to Sicily before being launched two to three miles offshore.

[12] Samuel W. Mitcham Jr. and Friedrich von Stauffenberg, *The Battle of Sicily: How the Allies Lost their Chance for Total Victory* (New York: Orion Books, 1991), p. 63.

[13] Mitcham Jr. and von Stauffenberg, *The Battle of Sicily*, p. 307.

[14] The ground forces for the Eastern Task Force were also known as the British Eighth Army while the US Western Task Force was also known as the US Seventh Army. General Alexander's combined Operation Husky army was thus termed the Fifteenth Army. Britain had previously fought the Tunisian War as the Eighteenth Army, its components being General Anderson's First Army and General Montgomery's Eighth Army. Confusingly, some primary sources mix up these designations, particularly when it comes to administration and maintenance in Sicily.

[15] Molony, *The Mediterranean and Middle East*, V, 130-131, 133.

[16] Carlo D'Este, *Bitter Victory: The Battle for Sicily, 1943* (New York: William Collins Sons and Co. Ltd., 1988: repr. 2008), p. 88.

[17] Up until 1984, British Army staff had three branches; A branch - responsible for all aspects of personnel management; G branch – divided into G.S. Intelligence and G.S. Operations and Training; Q branch – the quartermaster or logistics branch, divided into Q (Maintenance) responsible for provision of all materiel and Q (Movements) responsible for all transportation.

[18] Hugh Pond, *Sicily* (London: William Kimber, 1962), p. 29.

[19] Pond, *Sicily*, p. 31.

[20] Garland and McGaw Smyth, *The Mediterranean Theatre of Operations*, p. 1.

[21] London, Kings College London Liddell Hart Centre for Military Archives (KCLMA), GB0099 Alanbrooke, 6/7/4, Operation 'Symbol', Brigadier E.I.C. Jacob, 14.1.43, Brigadier Ian Jacob was the Military Assistant Secretary to the War Cabinet for the duration of the Second World War. His personal war diary, including the section written during the Symbol conference, is contained in the Alanbrooke collection.

[22] The Combined Chiefs of Staff (CCS) consisted of the British and American Chiefs of Staff (COS) sitting together. The CCS was based in Washington and the British COS were represented there by the principals of the British Joint Staff Mission. It was agreed that 'Joint' denoted inter-service collaboration, and 'Combined' applied to collaboration between two or more of the United Nations. In practice, the United States COS came to be known as the Joint COS and the British remained the British COS.

[23] KCLMA, GB0099 Alanbrooke 6/1/1, Casablanca Conference minutes, Directive to Commander-In-Chief, Allied Expeditionary Force in North Africa, Operation Husky 171/1/D, p. 127.

[24] James Willard, *General George S. Patton, Jr: Men Under Mars* (New York: Dodd, Mead & Company, 1946), p. 106.

[25] TNA, AIR 8/1344, Operation 'Husky', Report by the Joint Planning Staff, January 10 1943, Map C.

[26] TNA, AIR 23/6564, Operation 'Torch': report on

impressions gained from the assault stage.

[27] Pond, *Sicily*, p. 43.

[28] Force 141 was the team which was established to plan Operation Husky. It was formed on 10 February 1943 and reported to General Alexander, the DC-in-C.

[29] Geoffrey Perret, *Eisenhower* (New York: Random House, 1999), p. 206.

[30] Dwight D. Eisenhower, *Crusade in Europe* (London: Heinemann, 1948), p. 180.

[31] KCLMA, GB0099 Alanbrooke 6/2/22, correspondence between Montgomery and Alanbrooke, 12 April 1943.

[32] TNA, WO 106/3886, 'The Conquest of Sicily': despatch by Field Marshall Alexander, p. 9.

[33] TNA, CAB 44/124, Map A – The Actual Assaults of the Eighth Army and the dispositions as known at 2359hrs, 10 July 1943.

[34] TNA, WO 106/3886, 'The Conquest of Sicily': despatch by Field Marshall Alexander, Map 3.

[35] TNA, WO 106/3886, 'The Conquest of Sicily': despatch by Field Marshall Alexander, Map 4.

[36] Albert Kesselring, *The Memoirs of Field Marshall Kesselring* (London: William Kimber, 1953), p. 165.

[37] Kesselring, *The Memoirs of Field Marshall Kesselring*, p. 165.

[38] TNA, WO 106/3886, The Conquest of Sicily: despatch by Field Marshall Alexander, Map 5.

[39] Ken Ford, *Assault on Sicily: Monty and Patton at War* (Stroud: Sutton Publishing, 2007).

[40] Ian Gooderson, *A Hard Way to Make a War - The Allied Campaign in Italy in the Second World War* (London: Conway, 2008), p. 59.

[41] W. Craven and J. Cate, *The Army Air Forces in World War II,* 7vols (Chicago: University of Chicago Press, 1949), II.

[42] S. E. Morison, *History of United States Naval Operations in World War II,* 15 vols (Boston: Little, Brown, 1954), IX.

[43] Craven and Cate, *The Army Air Forces in World War II*, II, 445.

[44] Morison, *History of United States Naval Operations in*

World War II, IX, 30-33.

[45] Morison, *History of United States Naval Operations in World War II*, IX, 22.

[46] S. W. Roskill, *The War at Sea 1939-1945*, 3 vols (Uckfield: The Naval & Military Press, 1960), III.

[47] Molony, *The Mediterranean and Middle East*, V, xviii, 130-146.

[48] The Canadian Military History Headquarters (CMHQ) reports are a comprehensive collection of reports researched and written by Canadian military historical officers, based in London between 1940 and 1948. Colonel C. P. Stacey was appointed as the Canadian Historical Officer in October 1940. These reports have been declassified and are being placed online progressively over time and are a rich source of archival material.

[49] Canadian Military Headquarters (CMHQ) Reports, CMHQ Report #136, Canadian Operations in Sicily, July - August 1943. Part II: The Execution of the Operation by 1 Cdn Inf Div, Section 3, Special Aspects of the Sicilian Campaign, Introductory, p. 1.

[50] C. B. A. Behrens, *Merchant Shipping and the Demands of War* (London: Her Majesty's Stationery Office, 1978).

[51] Behrens, *Merchant Shipping and the Demands of War*, p. 330.

[52] Michael Howard, *Grand Strategy*, 6 vols (London, Her Majesty's Stationery Office, 1972), IV.

[53] Howard, *Grand Strategy*, IV, 360-361.

[54] Maurice Matloff, *Strategic Planning for Coalition Warfare, 1943-1944* (Washington: Center of Military History United States Army, 1959), p. 21.

[55] Howard, *Grand Strategy*, IV, 361-362.

[56] Hugh Pond, *Sicily* (London: Kimber 1962).

[57] Pond, *Sicily*, p. 211.

[58] Martin Blumenson, *Sicily: Whose Victory?* (New York: Ballantine, 1968).

[59] Blumenson, *Sicily*, p. 158.

[60] D'Este, *Bitter Victory*, p. 548.

[61] Rick Atkinson, *The Day of Battle: The War in Sicily and*

Italy, 1943-44 (London: Abacus, 2007; repr. 2014).

[62] Atkinson, *The Day of Battle*, pp. 58-59.

[63] Ian Blackwell, *The Battle for Sicily: Stepping Stone to Victory* (Barnsley: Pen and Sword, 2008).

[64] Blackwell, *The Battle for Sicily*, p. 196.

[65] Mitcham Jr. and von Stauffenberg, *The Battle of Sicily*, p. x.

[66] Mitcham Jr. and von Stauffenberg, *The Battle of Sicily*, p. 283.

[67] Martin Van Creveld, *Supplying War: Logistics from Wallenstein to Patton* (Cambridge: Cambridge University Press, 1977; repr. 2004).

[68] Van Creveld, *Supplying War*, pp. 231-232.

[69] William B. Breuer, *Drop Zone Sicily: Allied Airborne Strike, July 1943* (Novato, Calif.: Presidio Press, 1983: repr. 1997).

[70] Dr. John C. Warren, 'Airborne Missions in the Mediterranean 1942-1945' (unpublished doctoral thesis, USAF Historical Division, Maxwell, Al., 1955), p. 54.

[71] Warren, 'Airborne Missions in the Mediterranean 1942-1945', pp. 58-59.

[72] Stephen R. Cote, 'Operation Husky: A Critical Analysis' (unpublished doctoral thesis, Naval War College, Newport, R.I., 2001).

[73] Cote, 'Operation Husky', p. 15.

[74] Trevor Stone, 'Many Roads, Many Bridges: An analysis of the logistical support of the British 2nd Tactical Air Force during the Allied advance from Normandy 1944-1945' (unpublished Master's thesis, University of Buckingham, 2019).

[75] Stone, 'Many Roads, Many Bridges', p. 34.

[76] Arthur Tedder, *With Prejudice: The World War II Memoirs of Marshall of the Air Force Lord Tedder* (London: Cassell, 1966), p. 431. Cable from Montgomery to Alanbrooke, 19 April 1943

[77] TNA, AIR 8/1344, Operation Husky, Report by the Joint Planning Staff, J.P. (43) 7 (Final), January 10, 1943.

[78] G. W. L. Nicholson, *Official History of the Canadian Army in the Second World War: The Canadians in Italy 1943-*

45 (Ottowa: Edmond Cloutier, 1956), II, 13.

[79] TNA, AIR 8/1344, Operation Husky, Report by the Joint Planning Staff, J.P. (43) 7 (Final), January 10, 1943, p. 1.

[80] D'Este, *Bitter Victory*, pp. 604-609.

[81] TNA, WO 106/3886, 'The Conquest of Sicily': despatch by Field Marshall Alexander. Enemy Strength and Dispositions, p. 17.

[82] Molony, *The Mediterranean and Middle East,* V, 30.

[83] KCLMA, GB0099 Laycock, 5/22, memo Col. A. H. Head to C.G.S. 141, 13 June 1943.

[84] *Shore-to-shore* – assault forces transported from embarkation ports and then troops disembarked to beaches directly from beached craft.

[85] TNA, CAB 106/705, Sicily: despatch on the invasion 1943 July, by Admiral of the Fleet Sir Andrew B. Cunningham, Commander-in-Chief, Mediterranean.

[86] KCLMA, GB0099 Alanbrooke, 6/1/1-2, Casablanca Conference, p. 63.

[87] TNA, AIR 8/1344, Operation Husky, Report by the Joint Planning Staff, J.P. (43) 7 (Final), January 10, 1943, p. 2.

[88] TNA, AIR 8/1344, Operation Husky, Report by the Joint Planning Staff, J.P. (43) 7 (Final), January 10, 1943, Appendix F Maintenance, pp. 24-25.

[89] TNA, AIR 8/1344, Operation Husky, Report by the Joint Planning Staff, J.P. (43) 7 (Final), January 10, 1943, p. 25.

[90] TNA, AIR 8/1344, Operation Husky, Report by the Joint Planning Staff, J.P. (43) 7 (Final), January 10, 1943, p. 25.

[91] Molony, *The Mediterranean and Middle East,* V, 12.

[92] *Ship-to-shore* - assault forces transported to just offshore of target beaches with troops then embarked on specialised landing craft for short trip to beaches.

[93] TNA, CAB 44/165, Section 6, Chapter L, Part I, Section 4, Twelfth Army – Administrative Planning Instruction No. 1, Point 79, Tentage and Anti-Mosquito Protection, p. 81, 86. This file is a valuable archival source for researching the logistics of Operation Husky. Pessell draws on thirty-seven separate war diaries of the various HQs, Army Corps, Army Divisions, Beach Bricks, and transport convoys involved in

the campaign.

[94] KCLMA, GB0099 Alanbrooke, 6/2/23, correspondence between Montgomery and Alanbrooke, 6 May 1943.

[95] KCLMA, GB0099 Gale 2/1-2/13, Diary entries 2 and 3 May 1943.

[96] Molony, *The Mediterranean and Middle East,* V, 10.

[97] TNA, CAB 44/165, Section 6, Chapter L: Sicily; planning and maintenance 1943, pp. 1-3.

[98] Molony, *The Mediterranean and Middle East,* V, 4-5.

[99] Garland and McGaw Smyth, *The Mediterranean Theatre of Operations*, p. 11.

[100] KCMLA, GB0099 Alanbrooke, 6/2/17, 6 April 1943 - Letter PM to Alanbrooke.

[101] TNA, AIR 23/3345, History of AFHQ, Part II, Section III, pp. 357-359.

[102] Matthew Jones, *Britain, the United States and the Mediterranean War, 1942-44* (London: Macmillan Press, 1996), p. 58.

[103] KCLMA, GB0099 Gale 2/1-2/13.

[104] TNA, CAB 44/165, Section 6, Chapter L, Part I, Section 1, Diagram 1.

[105] TNA, CAB 106/705, Sicily: despatch on the invasion 1943 July, by Admiral of the Fleet Sir Andrew B. Cunningham, Commander-in-Chief, Mediterranean, Location of Headquarters.

[106] Blackwell, *The Battle for Sicily*, p. 50.

[107] Molony, *The Mediterranean and Middle East,* V, 6, 8.

[108] London, Imperial War Museum (IWM), Gairdner, 12979. The travel schedule referred to was calculated using Gairdner's diary entries.

[109] IWM, Gairdner, 12979, p. 17.

[110] KCLMA, GB0099 Gale 2/1-2/13, Diary entry 2 March 1943.

[111] KCLMA, GB0099 Gale 2/1-2/13, Diary entry 20 April 1943.

[112] Frederick Morgan, *Peace and War: A Soldier's Life* (London: Hodder and Stoughton, 1961).

[113] KCLMA, GB0099 Alanbrooke 6/2/23, p. 2.

114 TNA, AIR 23/5759, Invasion of Sicily: planning, p. 1.

115 Molony, *The Mediterranean and Middle East,* V, 5, footnote.

The evolution of the North African campaign helps illustrate the challenge faced by Husky commanders:

February 14th-26th approx. Axis offensives in central Tunisia.
20th Eighteenth Army Group constituted.

March

6th	Battle of Medenine.
20th-27th	Battle of Mareth.

April

6th	Battle of Wadi Akarit.
8th-16th	First Army on the offensive.
22nd	Beginning of general offensive to

destroy Axis forces in Tunisia.

May

6th	Final assault on Tunis and Bizerta.
13th	Enemy resistance ceases in Africa.

116 KCLMA, CGB0099 Alanbrooke, 6/2/22, correspondence between Montgomery and Alanbrooke, 19 April 1943.

117 TNA, WO 106/3886, The Conquest of Sicily: despatch by Field Marshall Alexander, p. 1.

118 KCLMA, CGB0099 Alanbrooke, 6/2/17, correspondence between Alexander and Alanbrooke, 5 April 1943.

119 KCLMA, GB0099 Alanbrooke, 6/2/46, correspondence between Maitland-Wilson and Alanbrooke, 1 April 1943.

120 KCMLA, GB0099 Alanbrooke, 6/2/22, correspondence between Montgomery and Alanbrooke, 12 April 1943.

121 KCLMA, CGB0099 Alanbrooke, 6/2/23, correspondence between Montgomery and Alanbrooke, 6 May 1943.

122 IWM, Gairdner 12979, entry 24 May 1943.

123 Jones, *Britain, the United States and the Mediterranean War, 1942-44*, p. 61.

124 IWM, Gairdner 12979, diary entry 22 February 1943.

125 Omar Bradley and Clay Blair, *A General's Life* (New York: Simon and Schuster, 1983), p. 198.

126 Molony, *The Mediterranean and Middle East,* V, 24.

127 KCLMA, GB0099 Alanbrooke, 6/2/22, correspondence

167

between Montgomery and Alanbrooke, 30 April 1943. Montgomery writes that 'As far as I can make out the trouble with Husky has been that no experienced fighting commander ever even read the proposed plan made out by the Planning Staff in London. And yet Algiers accepted in toto. This is really quite frightful'.

[128] The Canadian forces deployed in Sicily as part of the ETF were collectively badged as the 1st Canadian Infantry Division (often referred to as the First Canadian Infantry Division, or even the First Infantry Division, in Canadian and British Archives). This division comprised the 1 Canadian Infantry Brigade, the 2 Canadian Infantry Brigade, the 3 Canadian Infantry Brigade, the 1 Canadian Tank Brigade and various infantry support battalions as well as the Royal Canadian Engineers.

[129] CMHQ Report #126, Canadian Operations in Sicily, July - August 1943. Part I: The Preliminaries of OPERATION HUSKY (The Assault on Sicily), General Introduction, (b) Beginnings of Canadian Participation in Operation Husky (Paras 15-23), pp. 4-7.

[130] CMHQ Reports, Report #126, Canadian Operations in Sicily, July - August 1943. Part I: The Preliminaries of OPERATION HUSKY (The Assault on Sicily), Canadian Planning and Training, (b) The 1st Canadian Infantry Division Takes Over (Paras 66-76), pp. 24-25.

[131] CMHQ Report #126, Canadian Operations in Sicily, July - August 1943. Part I: The Preliminaries of OPERATION HUSKY (The Assault on Sicily), Canadian Planning and Training, (c) The CAIRO Visit: The Death of Major-General Salmon and Appointment of Major-General Simonds (Paras 77-96), p. 28.

[132] CMHQ Report #126, Canadian Operations in Sicily, July - August 1943. Part I: The Preliminaries of OPERATION HUSKY (The Assault on Sicily), Canadian Planning and Training, (d) A & Q Aspects of the Planning (Paras 97-135), pp. 38-39.

[133] TNA, CAB 44/165, Section 6, Chapter L, Section 6, 13 and 30 Corps - Administrative Plans and Instructions, (b) 30 Corps

– 1 Canadian Infantry Division, p. 100.

[134] CMHQ Report #136, Canadian Operations in Sicily, July - August 1943. Part II: The Execution of the Operation by 1 Cdn Inf Div, Section 3, Special Aspects of the Sicilian Campaign, (d) Signals, p. 5.

[135] CMHQ Report #126, Canadian Operations in Sicily, July - August 1943. Part I: The Preliminaries of OPERATION HUSKY (The Assault on Sicily), Canadian Planning and Training, (c) The CAIRO Visit: The Death of Major-General Salmon and the appointment of Major-General Simonds (Paras 77-96), p. 36. Another disaster nearly befell Simonds and his senior colleagues as they flew back to the United Kingdom from Cairo. Major A. F. B. Knight (DA&QMG, Canadian Planning Staff) wrote in his notes for DA&QMG War Diary: 'A near catastrophe. If it had not been for the excellent map reading of Maj.Gen. Simonds, we would have landed in Ireland and been interned. Fortunately, the poor navigation was noticed and it was pointed out to the navigator that we were over Ireland and NOT England, with the result that the course was changed.'

[136] Gropman, *The Big 'L': American Logistics in World War II*, p. 347.

[137] Behrens, *Merchant Shipping and the Demands of War*, p. 328.

[138] Howard, *Grand Strategy*, IV, 361.

[139] TNA, CAB 80/68/3, War Office Chiefs of Staff Committee, Note by Lt.-General Ismay, 22 March 1943, p. 169.

[140] TNA, CAB 80/68/3, War Office Chiefs of Staff Committee, Annex, Report by Lord Leathers, 22 March 1943, p. 170.

[141] Howard, *Grand Strategy*, IV, 360-361.

[142] TNA, CAB 80/68/4, War Cabinet COS Committee memo, Provision of Additional Landing Ships and Craft for Husky, 1 April 1943, pp. 247-250. TNA, CAB 80/68/5, War Cabinet COS Committee memo, Husky – Provision of Extra L.C.T., 4 April 1943, pp. 282-287.

[143] TNA, CAB 80/68/6, War Cabinet COS Committee memo, Provision of Additional Landing Ships and Craft for Husky, 11 April 1943, pp. 323-325

[144] KCLMA, GB0099 Alanbrooke 6/7/4, Brigadier E.I.C. Jacob conference diary, p. 44.

[145] D'Este, *Bitter Victory,* p. 51.

[146] KCLMA, GB0099 Alanbrooke 6/1/2, Trident Conference proceedings, pp. 38-42.

[147] KCLMA, GB0099 Alanbrooke 6/1/2, Trident Conference proceedings, p. 502.

[148] Garland and McGaw Smyth, *The Mediterranean Theatre of Operations*, pp. 23-24.

[149] Force 545 had in fact a cover designation of Twelfth Army, one of a number of deception plans for Operation Husky. It was an attempt to convince the Germans that twelve divisions were being assembled in the Middle East to invade Greece in order to hook up with the Russian Red Army. Many primary sources such as logistics plans, issued between 19 April and the end of the campaign, substitute Twelfth Army for Force 545.

[150] G-1 and G-4 branches were the American equivalents of the British A and Q branches.

[151] TNA, CAB 44/165, Section 6, Chapter L, Part I, Section 2, H.Q. Force 141 – Administrative appreciation and Outline Maintenance Project, p. 3.

[152] TNA, CAB 44/165, Section 6, Chapter L, Part I, Section 2, H.Q. Force 141 – Administrative appreciation and Outline Maintenance Project, p. 4.

[153] Molony, *The Mediterranean and Middle East,* V, 132.

[154] KCLMA, GB0099 Gale, 2/1-2/13, Memorandum from Gale to D.Q.M.G (War Office), 25 February 1943.

[155] *LofC Area* - a position on the LofC, organised under one authority for purposes of local administration. It might be divided into Sub-Areas which could function independently if the volume of work warranted it.

[156] TNA, CAB 44/165, Section 6, Chapter L, Part I, Section 1, H.Q. Force 141 – Administrative appreciation and Outline Maintenance Project, p. 2.

[157] TNA, CAB 44/165, Section 6, Chapter L, Part I, Section 2, H.Q. Force 141 – Administrative appreciation and Outline Maintenance Project, pp. 10-28.

[158] Bigot was an alternative code word which was often used instead of Husky.

[159] *Assault Scales* were calculated to meet all the needs of units and formations, enabling them to operate up to a depth of ten miles from their maintenance areas on the beach. *Light Scales* increased the Assault Scales so as to enable units and formations to operate up to a distance of thirty miles from the beach maintenance areas for a period of up to three weeks. *War Establishment* was the full wartime complement of units and formations of personnel, equipment and vehicles.

[160] TNA, CAB 44/165, Section 6, Chapter L, Part I, Section 2, H.Q. Force 141 – Third Outline Maintenance Project, pp. 14-18.

[161] TNA, CAB 44/165, Section 6, Chapter L, Part I, Section 4, Twelfth Army – Administrative Planning Instruction No. 1, pp. 71-93.

[162] TNA, CAB 44/165, Section 6, Chapter L, Part I, Section 4, Twelfth Army – Administrative Planning Instruction No. 1, Appendix H, Documents Required by Mov & Tn, p. 89.

[163] *First Line Transport* - Minimum transport capability that an assault unit needed to have available to it. *Second Line Transport* - Transport capability, normally 3-ton trucks, which could move divisions or brigade groups and their ammunition and supplies. *Third Line Transport* - Transport capability, normally under the control of an Army or Corps, for any purpose that circumstances might require.

[164] TNA, CAB 44/165, Section 6, Chapter L, Part I, Section 4, Twelfth Army – Administrative Planning Instruction No. 1, Point 48, Rations, pp. 77-78.

[165] *AFV* - Armoured Fighting Vehicles. *MT* – Mechanical Transport.

[166] TNA, CAB 44/165, Section 6, Chapter L, Part I, Section 4, Twelfth Army – Administrative Planning Instruction No. 1, Appendix K, Combined Operations, Waterproofing of Vehicles and Equipment, pp. 91-92.

[167] Molony, *The Mediterranean and Middle East,* V, 143. HQ 86 LofC Area, commanded by Brigadier H. C. N. Trollope, has been described as becoming 'almost the 8th Army's

administrative assault-force in the days of the advance to Tripoli in January 1943'. They were to fulfil this role again for the ETF in Operation Husky.

[168] TNA, CAB 44/165, Section 6, Chapter L, Part I, Section 5, Twelfth Army – Administrative Planning Instruction No. 2, Section 5, p. 95.

[169] TNA, CAB 107/135, Husky: Lessons from operation: report on beach maintenance in Sicily, Part III – Preparation and Planning, Section 5, Multiple Responsibility for Mounting the Force, p. 4.

[170] TNA, CAB 44/165, Section 6, Chapter L, Part I, Section 5, Twelfth Army – Administrative Planning Instruction No. 2, Section 6, pp. 96-97.

[171] TNA, CAB 44/165, Section 6, Chapter L, Part I, Section 9, The Mounting of Husky in the Middle East: Planning and Execution of Moves, pp. 109-122.

[172] TNA, CAB 44/165, Section 6, Chapter L, Part I, Section 9, The Mounting of Husky in the Middle East: Planning and Execution of Moves, pp. 109-122.

[173] TNA, CAB 44/165, Section 6, Chapter L, Part I, Section 9, The Mounting of Husky in the Middle East: Planning and Execution of Moves, Appendix IV, Personnel and Stores Moved to and Embarked at Middle East Ports for Husky, Loading, p. 111.

[174] TNA, CAB 44/165, Section 6, Chapter L, Part I, Section 9, The Mounting of Husky in the Middle East: Planning and Execution of Moves, Appendix IV, Personnel and Stores Moved to and Embarked at Middle East Ports for Husky, p. 113. These troop numbers included administrative personnel as well as assault troops.

[175] TNA, WO 204/7525, Lessons learned from training exercises, 12 July 1943, p. 4.

[176] KCLMA, GB0099 Alanbrooke, 6/2/22, correspondence between Montgomery and Alanbrooke, 19 April 1943.

[177] KCLMA, GB0099 Alanbrooke, 6/2/23, correspondence between Montgomery and Alanbrooke, 5 May 1943.

[178] TNA, CAB 80/68/1, War Office Chiefs of Staff Committee, memorandum no. 114, Piers for Use on Flat Beaches, 11

March 1943, pp. 47-50. This memorandum is of significance as it highlights Churchill's direct involvement in encouraging Mountbatten, the Chief of Combined Operations, to be more inventive in how he approached the problem of facilitating beach landings. Many of the techniques trialled at Husky would be used in Normandy in June 1944.

[179] *Operation Husky landing craft* (speed 8-10 knots):

LCA – Landing Craft Assault (thirty-five men);

LCF – Landing Craft Flak, anti-aircraft (500 tons);

LCG – Landing Craft Gun, carrying two 4.7 in guns (500 tons);

LCI – Landing Craft Infantry (200 men, 250 tons);

LCM – Landing Craft Mechanised (30 tons);

LCP – Landing Craft Personnel (9 tons);

LCS - Landing Craft Support;

LCT – Landing Craft Tank (300-350 tons);

LCT (R) – Landing Craft Rocket (500 tons).

Operation Husky landing ships (speed 8 knots and above):

LSI (L) – Landing Ship Infantry (Large) to carry LCAs;

LSI (M) - Landing Ship Infantry (Medium);

LSI (S) - Landing Ship Infantry (Small);

LST - Landing Ship Tank (2000 tons);

LSH - Landing Ship Headquarters (Communications Centre).

[180] TNA, WO 106/3875, Husky: Training, Cipher Telegram from G-3 signed Eisenhower to War Office, 13 March 1943.

[181] *DUKW* comes from General Motors Corporation model nomenclature:

D - designed in 1942;

U - utility;

K - all wheel drive;

W - dual tandem rear axles.

[182] CMHQ, Report #126, Canadian Operations in Sicily, July - August 1943. Part I: The Preliminaries of OPERATION HUSKY (The Assault on Sicily), Canadian Planning and Training, (d) A & Q Aspects of the Planning (Paras 97-135), p. 44. Of the 350 DUKWs allotted to the ETF, 100 were sent direct from the United States to the United Kingdom for the First Canadian Division. The consignment experienced

significant delays and, while they arrived just in time for embarkation, there was no time for the drivers to train in the usage of the vehicles.

[183] CMHQ, Report #126, Canadian Operations in Sicily, July - August 1943. Part I: The Preliminaries of OPERATION HUSKY (The Assault on Sicily), Embarkation, Exercise Stymie and the Voyage to Sicily (Paras 258-276), pp. 76-77. A full report on Exercise Stymie can be found in the Library and Archives Canada, File no. 233C1.075 (D3) Movement of 1 Cdn Inf Div to Sicily – Op Husky incl pers for embarkation after 15 Jun 43 and allocation to convoy - Husky/1 Cdn Inf Div/Q/H Doc I.

[184] TNA, CAB 44/165, Section 6, Chapter L, Part I, Section 9, The Mounting of Husky in the Middle East: Planning and Execution of Moves, Appendix IV, Exercises, p. 111.

[185] TNA, WO 106/3886, The Conquest of Sicily: despatch by Field Marshall Alexander, p. 14.

[186] TNA, WO 204/7525, Lessons learned from training exercises, 12 July 1943, Time Factors, p. 1.

[187] TNA, WO 106/3886, The Conquest of Sicily: despatch by Field Marshall Alexander, p. 14.

[188] Bernard Fergusson, *The Watery Maze: The Story of Combined Operations*, (London: Collins, 1961), p. 230. Sir Bernard Fergusson was Director of British Combined Operations from 1945 to 1946 and his book, published in 1961, chronicles the evolution of Combined Operations from its early beginnings, through the various amphibious operations in the Second World War, culminating in the Normandy invasion, and the challenges it faced as an inter-service organisation. He was given free access to documents, archives and minutes of meetings; however, the publication has no footnoting or referencing. Sir Bernard served as the Governor-General of New Zealand from 1962 to 1967.

[189] TNA, CAB 44/165, Section 6, Chapter L, Part I, Section 2, H.Q. Force 141 – Administrative appreciation and Outline Maintenance Project, p. 3.

[190] KCLMA, GB0099 Laycock, 5/22, memo Col. A. H. Head to C.G.S. 141, 13 June 1943.

[191] KCLMA, GB0099 Laycock, 5/22, letter from Lord Louis Mountbatten to Colonel A. H. Head, 13 March 1943.

[192] KCLMA, GB0099 Laycock, 5/22, memo Col. A. H. Head to C.G.S. 141, point (c), 13 June 1943.

[193] John Grehan and Martin Mace, *The War in Italy 1943-1944: Despatches from the Front* (Barnsley: Pen & Sword, 2014), p. 35. Also TNA, CAB 106/705, Sicily: despatch on the invasion 1943 July, by Admiral of the Fleet Sir Andrew B. Cunningham, Commander-in-Chief, Mediterranean.

[194] TNA, CAB 44/165, Section 6, Chapter L, Part I, Section 3, The Operational Plan Entirely Recast: Some Administrative Factors, Beach Groups and Beach Bricks, pp. 31-34.

[195] GHQ MEF called their beach organisations Beach Bricks while AFHQ and the War Office in London referred to them as Beach Groups. There were some subtle differences between each, for instance the Beach Bricks handled POL as well as rations, but they were fundamentally the same thing. A detailed comparison of the three Beach Group organisations and their differences can be found in TNA, CAB 107/135, Husky: Lessons from operation: report on beach maintenance in Sicily, Appendix B, Comparative Table of the Different Beach Group Organizations, p. 10.

[196] KCLMA, GB0099 Alanbrooke, 6/2/46, correspondence between Maitland-Wilson and Alanbrooke, 3 July 1943.

[197] Molony, *The Mediterranean and Middle East,* V, 140.

[198] TNA, WO 204/6982, Operation Husky: Beach Groups and maintenance Bricks organisation, Section 24B, Organisation of Beach Bricks. This archive contains comprehensive detail of the Middle East Beach Brick concept and its organisational evolution during the preparations for Operation Husky. Section 24B contains detailed organisation charts for Beach Bricks with the make-up of each unit split by service type and by personnel (total 2,830 men – 130 officers, 2,700 ordinary ranks).

[199] Molony, *The Mediterranean and Middle East,* V, 141. Distribution of Beach Groups and DUKWs.

[200] Molony, *The Mediterranean and Middle East,* V, 141.

[201] TNA, WO 252/1199, Beach intelligence reports: operation

Husky, Appendix M.

[202] TNA, WO, 106/3862, Operation Husky: Force 141: planning instructions, Planning Instruction No. 7, cover note from Major General C. H. Gairdner, 18 March 1943.

[203] CMHQ, Report #126, Canadian Operations in Sicily, July - August 1943. Part I: The Preliminaries of OPERATION HUSKY (The Assault on Sicily), Embarkation, Exercise Stymie and the Voyage to Sicily (Paras 258-276), pp. 79.

[204] Molony, *The Mediterranean and Middle East,* V, 50.

[205] Molony, *The Mediterranean and Middle East,* V, 50.

[206] TNA, ADM, 199/2515, Mounting the expedition in Eastern Mediterranean, Narrative of Events on the Levant Station leading up to Operation Husky, Admiral J.H.D. Cunningham, Appendix I, entry 6 February 1943.

[207] S. W. C. Pack, *Operation Husky: The Allied Invasion of Sicily* (Newton Abbot: David & Charles, 1977), p. 43. Captain S. W. C. Pack was an officer in the Royal Navy and worked with the CCS in Washington during the planning of Operation Husky, becoming a prolific author on maritime topics after the Second World War. In response to an appeal for material for his book on the invasion of Sicily, he received 270 individual accounts of experiences from those who participated in Husky. His book focusses on the naval aspects of the campaign and has primary source legitimacy, although there is no footnoting or referencing.

[208] TNA, WO 252/1199, Beach intelligence reports: operation Husky. This file is a catalogue of the beach reconnaissance data collected by the COPPs up to D-day. The process was ongoing with constant refinements being made to coastal maps as new information was discovered. The file contains maps, photographs and sketches as well as details of the submarine and COPP reconnaissance missions.

[209] Grehan and Mace, *The War in Italy 1943-1944: Despatches from the Front* (Barnsley: Pen & Sword, 2014), Admiral of the Fleet Sir Andrew B. Cunningham's Despatch on the Invasion of Sicily, p. 36.

[210] Pack, *Operation Husky*, p. 43.

[211] TNA, WO 106/3886, The Conquest of Sicily: despatch by

Field Marshall Alexander, footnote p. 15. Alexander says the Allies were able to discern the location of Italian units in Sicily by intercepting the post of the several hundred thousand Italian POWs captured in the Middle East and noting the unit address of Sicilian relations and friends in the services when they wrote to the POWs. The Italian censor was far less active than his German counterpart. 'It was very nearly our only source for the Italian Order of Battle and much the most copious. It could not be applied to the more efficient German security system.'

[212] CMHQ Report #127, Canadian Operations in Sicily, July - August 1943. Part II: The Execution of the operation by 1 Cdn Inf Div, Section 1, The Assault and Initial Penetration Inland, First Advance Inland and Capture of Pachino Airfield, Appendix A, Map of the Invasion of Sicily by 15 Army Group.

[213] TNA, CAB 44/165, Section 6, Chapter L, Part II, Section 17, Operational Maintenance and Administration of 13 and 30 Corps after the Assault Phase, p. 180.

[214] Christine Leppard, 'Documenting the D-Day Dodgers: Canadian Field Historians in the Italian Campaign, 1943-1945', Canadian Military History: Vol. 18: Iss. 3, Article 3. Leppard has written a comprehensive paper on the role of Canadian Field Historians in the Italian campaign, including the selection and experiences of Captain Sesia. Sesia was accompanied by a war artist, Lieutenant Will Ogilvie, charged with the task of recording the Canadian effort on canvas.

[215] TNA, CAB 44/165, Section 6, Chapter L, Part I, Section 6, 13 and 30 Corps - Administrative Plans and Instructions, (b) 30 Corps – 1 Canadian Infantry Division, p. 101.

[216] TNA, CAB 44/165, Section 6, Chapter L, Part I, Section 6, 13 and 30 Corps - Administrative Plans and Instructions, (b) 30 Corps – 1 Canadian Infantry Division, p. 98.

[217] TNA, CAB 44/165, Section 6, Chapter L, Part I, Section 6, 13 and 30 Corps – Administrative Plans and Instructions, (b) 30 Corps – 1 Canadian Infantry Division, pp. 102-103.

KMF18 (F for Fast) and KMS19 (S for Slow) were the Royal Navy designations for the convoys but confusingly they were also known as Force X and Force Y respectively.

[218] TNA, WO 107/135, Husky: Lessons from operation: report on beach maintenance in Sicily, Part II, Section 3, Preparation and Planning, Maintenance Policy, p. 3.

[219] TNA, CAB 44/165, Section 6, Chapter L, Part I, Section 6, 13 and 30 Corps - Administrative Plans and Instructions, (b) 30 Corps – 1 Canadian Infantry Division, pp. 103. This page contains a table which specifies a detailed composition of both convoys.

[220] TNA, CAB 44/165, Section 6, Chapter L, Part I, Section 13, (b) Convoy Losses before D day, pp. 153-154.

[221] CMHQ, Report #126, Canadian Operations in Sicily, July - August 1943. Part I: The Preliminaries of OPERATION HUSKY (The Assault on Sicily), Embarkation, Exercise Stymie and the Voyage to Sicily (Paras 258-276), pp. 79. A manifest of the vehicles and equipment lost is detailed in paragraph 270.

[222] TNA, CAB 44/165, Section 6, Chapter L, Part I, Section 13, (b) Convoy Losses before D day, p. 54.

[223] Molony, *The Mediterranean and Middle East,* V, 57. *Release Position* – larger assault vessels were guided towards release positions between two and seven miles offshore, marked by sonic buoys which had been placed underwater by beacon submarines on 9 July, which then surfaced on 10 July. At this point, troops would transfer to smaller landing craft, which had been transported onboard, for the final run to the beaches.

[224] CMHQ Report #126, Canadian Operations in Sicily, July - August 1943. Part I: The Preliminaries of OPERATION HUSKY (The Assault on Sicily), Appendix B Map of the Assault on Bark West Beach by 1 Cdn Inf Div.

[225] TNA, WO 107/135, Husky: Lessons from operation: report on beach maintenance in Sicily, Part II, Section 7, Available Information, (a) Beaches, p. 7.

[226] TNA, WO 107/135, Husky: Lessons from operation: report on beach maintenance in Sicily, Part III, Section 17, 4 Beach Group, p. 7.

[227] TNA, WO 107/135, Husky: Lessons from operation: report

on beach maintenance in Sicily, Part III, Section 11, Events after Landing, p. 5.

[228] CMHQ Report #126, Canadian Operations in Sicily, July - August 1943. Part I: The Preliminaries of OPERATION HUSKY (The Assault on Sicily), Appendix I, Message sent to HMS *Glengyle* on 7 July 1943 instructing the use of DUKWs for troop landings.

[229] TNA, CAB 44/165, Section 6, Chapter L, Part II, Section 14, The Assault Phase, p. 157.

[230] TNA, WO 107/135, Husky: Lessons from operation: report on beach maintenance in Sicily, Part III, Section 10, Initial Landing, p. 5.

[231] TNA, CAB 44/165, Section 6, Chapter L, Part II, Section 14, The Assault Phase, pp. 157-158.

[232] TNA, WO 107/135, Husky: Lessons from operation: report on beach maintenance in Sicily, Part IV, Section 16, 3 Beach Group, p. 6. Sommerfeld Tracking, named after a German expatriate engineer living in England, was a lightweight wire mesh surface reinforced laterally by steel rods. It was typically used as a temporary prefabricated airfield surface but was also deployed for beach landings.

[233] TNA, WO 107/135, Husky: Lessons from operation: report on beach maintenance in Sicily, Part VI, Amphibian DUKWs, Section 38, Appreciation, p. 18.

[234] TNA, WO 107/135, Husky: Lessons from operation: report on beach maintenance in Sicily, Part XIV, Maps – Corps First Key Plan, p. 37.

[235] TNA, CAB 44/165, Section 6, Chapter L, Part II, Section 14, The Assault Phase, p. 158.

[236] TNA, WO 107/135, Husky: Lessons from operation: report on beach maintenance in Sicily, Part III, Section 13, Final Key Plan, p. 6.

[237] TNA, WO 107/135, Husky: Lessons from operation: report on beach maintenance in Sicily, Part IV, Section 17, 4 Beach Group, p. 7. The logisticians had a balance to strike with respect to the value of using prisoners of war from D+1 to D+14 when set against the need to feed them. The non-delivery of ration stores over Beach 57 on D-day had created a

shortage of food for front line troops (see CMHQ Report #126, 53 (g), p. 25.

238 TNA, WO 107/135, Husky: Lessons from operation: report on beach maintenance in Sicily, Part IV, Appendix C, 4 Beach Group - Vehicles and Stores discharged at Bark South daily, p. 11. Appendix D includes a day-by-day breakdown of the nature of the stores received (Supplies, Water, POL, Ammunition, Ordnance Stores, Royal Engineer Stores) as well as stores issued into the supply chain.

239 TNA, WO 107/135, Husky: Lessons from operation: report on beach maintenance in Sicily, Part XIV, Maps – Corps Final Key Plan, p. 38.

240 TNA, WO 107/135, Husky: Lessons from operation: report on beach maintenance in Sicily, Part XII, Conclusion, p. 32.

241 TNA, WO 107/135, Husky: Lessons from operation: report on beach maintenance in Sicily, Part VII, Beach Depots, pp. 24-26.

242 TNA, CAB 44/165, Section 6, Chapter L, Part II, Section 15, The Maintenance Situation of Eighth Army at the end of July 1943, p. 171. Logisticians also had to make allowances for shipping losses throughout the campaign. From D-day to D+14, 97,64 tons of stores were lost in shipping by enemy action, equal to ten per cent of 98,636 tons shipped, leaving 88,872 tons landed. In the same period 1,181 vehicles were lost out of a total of 12,556 shipped.

243 TNA, WO 107/135, Husky: Lessons from operation: report on beach maintenance in Sicily, Part XI, Summary (g), p. 32.

244 TNA, WO 107/135, Husky: Lessons from operation: report on beach maintenance in Sicily, Part I, Introduction, p. 3.

245 CMHQ Report #136, Canadian Operations in Sicily, July - August 1943. Part II: The Execution of the operation by 1 Cdn Inf Div, Section 3, Special Aspects of the Sicilian Campaign, The A and Q Part in the Sicilian Campaign (paras 21-38), pp. 8-13.

246 CMHQ Report #136, Canadian Operations in Sicily, July - August 1943. Part II: The Execution of the operation by 1 Cdn Inf Div, Section 3, Special Aspects of the Sicilian Campaign, The A and Q Part in the Sicilian Campaign (paras 21-38), p. 9.

[247] Molony, *The Mediterranean and Middle East,* V, 137.

[248] CMHQ Report #136, Canadian Operations in Sicily, July - August 1943. Part II: The Execution of the operation by 1 Cdn Inf Div, Section 3, Special Aspects of the Sicilian Campaign, The A and Q Part in the Sicilian Campaign (paras 21-38), (a) Service Corps, pp. 14-15. Mules and horses were requisitioned from locals without any form of contract or even a price being agreed. Requisition notes were issued and the owners were told to contact AMGOT to secure reparation. TNA, CAB 44/165, Section 6, Chapter L, Part I, Section 6, 13 and 30 Corps – Administrative Plans and Instructions, (b) 30 Corps, p. 100. In March 1943 the War Office had stressed the importance of pack transport to cope with the mountainous terrain in Sicily and the First Canadian Division took with it an ex-cavalry officer and some other ranks who were experienced in mule pack transport, together with 100 sets of pack saddlery and equipment.

[249] *Forward Maintenance Centre* – a location at the leading edge of a LofC, radiating from a base depot, where supplies, equipment and ammunition could be accumulated close to a battle front.

[250] CMHQ Report #136, Canadian Operations in Sicily, July - August 1943. Part II: The Execution of the operation by 1 Cdn Inf Div, Section 3, Special Aspects of the Sicilian Campaign, The A and Q Part in the Sicilian Campaign (paras 21-38), (a) Service Corps, pp. 13-14.

[251] TNA, WO 107/135, Husky: Lessons from operation: report on beach maintenance in Sicily, Part XIV, Map IV, Progress of the Advance, p. 39.

[252] The Allied invasion of mainland Italy in September by Alexander's Fifteenth Army was made up of three separate assaults: an amphibious landing at Reggio Di Calabria on 3 September (Operation Baytown) by Montgomery's Eighth Army; an unopposed disembarkation at Taranto on 9 September (Operation Slapstick) by British First Airborne Division and an amphibious landing at Salerno on 9 September (Operation Avalanche) by General Mark W. Clark's Fifth Army.

[253] CMHQ Report #127, Canadian Operations in Sicily, July - August 1943. Part II: The Execution of the operation by 1 Cdn Inf Div, Section 1, The Assault and Initial Penetration Inland, First Advance Inland and Capture of Pachino Airfield (paras16-22), pp. 5-6.

[254] TNA, CAB 44/165, Section 6, Chapter L, Part II, Section 14, The Assault Phase, p. 162.

[255] TNA, CAB 44/165, Section 6, Chapter L, Part II, Section 14, The Assault Phase, p. 167. On 20 July (D+10), the WTF told HQ Fifteenth Army Group that they did not need this extra tonnage as the US beaches, plus the small ports of Licata and Porto Empedocle, were capable of satisfying all the WTF's needs. On 22 July, the WTF captured Palermo and its axis of supply was transferred to the large, deep-water port there.

[256] TNA, CAB 44/165, Section 6, Chapter L, Part II, Section 14, The Assault Phase, pp. 158-159.

[257] TNA, WO 106/3886, The Conquest of Sicily: despatch by Field Marshall Alexander. Summary of Logistical Information, 5. Discharges, p.110.

[258] TNA, CAB 44/165, Section 6, Chapter L, Part II, Section 17, Operational Maintenance and Administration of 13 and 30 Corps after the Assault Phase, p. 170. Daily drawings of ammunition by 13 Corps formations were restricted on 22 July and again on 26 July owing to logistical misunderstandings, but the FMC serving these formations was then moved from Syracuse to Lentini thirty-five miles north which successfully addressed the supply shortfall.

[259] TNA, CAB 44/165, Section 6, Chapter L, Part II, Section 17, Operational Maintenance and Administration of 13 and 30 Corps after the Assault Phase, Appendix VI, H.Q. 30 Corps Adm. Order No. 89, pp. 183-187.

[260] TNA, CAB 44/165, Section 6, Chapter L, Part II, Section 14, The Assault Phase, p. 163.

[261] TNA, CAB 44/165, Section 6, Chapter L, Part II, Section 14, The Assault Phase, pp. 163-164.

[262] TNA, CAB 44/165, Section 6, Chapter L, Part II, Section 21, Map Fortbase and the L of C Eighth Army, p. 205.

263 TNA, CAB 44/165, Section 6, Chapter L, Part II, Section 14, The Assault Phase, pp. 167-168.

264 TNA, CAB 44/165, Section 6, Chapter L, Part II, Section 16, H.Q. Eighth Army: August 1943. Railway Development and Final Administrative Instruction, pp. 172-173.

265 TNA, CAB 44/165, Section 6, Chapter L, Part II, Section 20, The Working of the Beaches in Sicily, p. 201.

266 There were numerous after-action reports commissioned to identify lessons learned from Operation Husky. The principal ones contained in the primary archives are: TNA, ADM 199/2509, Report of Eastern Task Force (Vice Admiral Ramsay); TNA, ADM 199/2510, Report of Western Task Force (Vice Admiral Hewitt); TNA, ADM 199/2515, Mounting the Expedition in the Eastern Mediterranean (Admiral Cunningham); TNA, AIR 23/6564, Operation 'Torch': report on impressions gained from the assault stage; TNA, WO 107/135, Husky: Lessons from operation: report on beach maintenance in Sicily; TNA, WO 201/660, Husky: 8th Army first report and lessons; TNA, WO 204/1906, Tactical lessons from the Sicilian campaign; TNA, WO 204/6021, COHQ Notes on U.S. Planning and Assault Phases of Operation Husky - by a British Military Observer; TNA, WO 204/6898, Lessons learned from the Sicilian campaign: A.F.H.Q Training Memorandum; TNA, WO 204/7525, Lessons learned from training exercises; TNA, WO 204/7546, Fortbase: administrative lessons learned.

267 KCLMA, GB0099 Gale 2/1-2/13, Letter Eisenhower to Gale, 20 August 1943.

268 Winston S. Churchill, *The River War: An Historical Account of the Reconquest of the Soudan* (London: Longmans, Green and Co., 1899), I, 275-276.

269 Helmuth Graf von Moltke and Daniel J. Hughes, *Moltke on the Art of War: Selected Writings* (New York: Random House, 1993), p. 92.

270 KCLMA, GB0099 Alanbrooke 6/1/1, Casablanca Conference Papers, System of Command for Combined U.S.-British operations, pp. 1-4.

[271] TNA, CAB 44/165, Section 6, Chapter L, Part I, Section 4, Twelfth Army – Administrative Planning Instruction No. 1, Appendix A and B, Provisional Allotment of Shipping to Destinations, pp. 83-85

[272] TNA, CAB 44/165, Section 6, Chapter L, Part I, Section 4, Twelfth Army – Administrative Planning Instruction No. 1, Appendix E, Special Commodities, p. 86.

[273] TNA, CAB 44/165, Section 6, Chapter L, Part I, Section 9, The Mounting of Husky in the M.E. – Planning and Execution of Moves, Appendix IV, pp. 113-122.

[274] TNA, WO 107/135, Husky: Lessons from operation: report on beach maintenance in Sicily, Part IV, Notes on the Working of Sub-Area and Beach Groups, Appendix B, Comparative Table of the Different Beach Organisations, p. 10.

[275] TNA, CAB 44/125, Section IV, Chapters D; The Advance to the Etna Line, 14 July – 12July 1943, by Major F. Jones, Order of Battle of British and Allied Formations, July 1943.

[276] TNA, WO 107/135, Husky: Lessons from operation: report on beach maintenance in Sicily, Part IV, Notes on the Working of Sub-Area and Beach Groups, Appendix A, 103 Beach Sub-Area, Summary of Position on Bark Beaches at 1700hrs daily, pp. 9, 11.

[277] TNA, CAB 44/165, Section 6, Chapter L, Part II, Section 19, H.Q. 15 Army Group – Weekly Administrative Review, August 1943, pp. 197-198.